ment, in the interests of entire accuracy, demands some qualification. I should say, I suppose, that I am in as good spirits as I can be under the distressing circumstances which have banished me temporarily from the sunshine of your presence. I can never, dear lady, be completely myself except with you.

And yet I beg you to believe that even my absence is intended to be in your interest quite as much as in the interest of any other person or any other cause. It is for you, as

(Continued in back)

PORTRAIT
OF A QUAKER

PORTRAIT
OF A QUAKER

Levi T. Pennington
(1875-1975)

A Critical Biography

By Donald McNichols
Professor of English
Seattle Pacific University

PORTRAIT OF A QUAKER

© Copyright 1980 by THE BARCLAY PRESS

International Standard Book Number: 0-913342-24-6

Library of Congress Catalog Card Number: 80-66654

First Printing, May 1980

Graphic design of cover by Stan Putman.

Cover photo of Levi T. Pennington at 91 years of age by Riley Studio, Newberg, Oregon.

Editing, composition, and lithography by The Barclay Press, Newberg, Oregon, United States of America.

⟳ Printed on Simpson 100% Recycled Text Paper

DEDICATED
TO

Lydia A. McNichols

and

Genette McNichols

Contents

Foreword

By Arthur O. Roberts

WORDS SHAPE OUR PERCEPTIONS of the world and mold them into lasting forms. The speakers and writers of society are craftsmen of these abiding forms. By this book the life of the late Levi Pennington is fashioned into a legacy. A master of the spoken word takes shape before our eyes in this work by a master of the written word, Donald McNichols.

Currently professor of English at Seattle Pacific University, McNichols served as dean of George Fox College from 1950 to 1955. He taught during those years, also, and is remembered fondly by many students for whom he opened doors of the spirit and the mind as well as pages of literature. This Quaker educator had been secured to provide academic direction at George Fox College, coming from Los Angeles Pacific College, where he had taught and administrated for a decade.

During the years 1952-54 McNichols served on the council that administered George Fox College interregnum. He was instrumental in securing Milo Ross for the presidency in 1954.

At George Fox College he became acquainted with Levi Pennington himself, as well as with the college and the church that Pennington had shaped so significantly.

When I arrived in Newberg from Boston in the fall of 1953 to begin a teaching career at George Fox College, there were fewer than one hundred students, the salary was wholly inadequate, and the facilities substandard. But there was a man with a vision of what Christian higher education ought to be. (Two decades later this concept would be labeled "faith and learning.") What I had learned from Gervas Carey and from George Moore while a student at the college about the unity of God's truth I found reiterated by Dean McNichols. During the year I was recruited it impressed me that in this problem-ridden school its dean had fostered a scholarly publication, the George Fox "Journal." For many years subsequently the "Journal" printed and circulated the annual faculty lecture. In an early issue entitled "What Is an Adequate College?" McNichols wrote:

> . . . the program at George Fox attempts to recognize its responsibility as a liberal arts college through earnestness of academic endeavor and honesty toward truth. As a Christian college it seeks to express the highest in Christian idealism, and as a Quaker college it attempts to remind its students that first they should discover the immediate experience of God, then proceed to study man's discoveries.

Donald McNichols provided a hinge between classical nineteenth century Christian orthodoxy, represented by young Levi Pennington setting forth to administer a struggling Quaker college in Oregon in 1911, and midtwentieth century Christian orthodoxy arising out of World War II's rubble of broken polarities and shattered superficialities. The work of the pioneers is perfected by those who more fully, but with the same faith, enter the vision.

The Quakers have a query aimed at reflective introspection, "When differences arise, are efforts made to end them speedily?" The ameliorative administrative efforts of Donald McNichols in the past are advanced by the insights of this book. Although some of the differences among Friends, in which Levi Pennington inevitably played a significant role, may seem to have been extensive in duration, yet from the perspective of history the restoration of wholeness to a church body and the healing of personal hurts took place quite rapidly.

The inclusion of Pennington's prayers serves as a reminder that in worship Christ draws us together, in truth and in love, to the place from which words come—whether spoken or written.

Acknowledgments

I WISH TO ACKNOWLEDGE indebtedness to those who assisted me in this project by their encouragement, their expressions of sincere interest, and their statements of confidence. This list is long, including my writing students, colleagues, and family.

Dr. Elton Trueblood gave me the first words of encouragement, outside of my family, and he kindly recommended me to Mary (Pennington) Pearson, who approved my undertaking the task of writing a biography of her father.

A special word of appreciation is due Seattle Pacific University in approving this effort as a part of my professional growth and development plan in writing, and for granting me a sabbatical leave for the writing stage.

For access to private papers, I am indebted to the Special Collections Division, University of Oregon Library; The Quaker Collection and archives of Shambaugh Library; and the family papers in the possession of Dr. Pennington's granddaughter Bertha May Nicholson.

Finally I express appreciation to a number of people who have aided me in a number of ways: to my wife Lydia who, among other things, cheerfully permitted the family room to serve as a second study devoted only to the files for this project; to my sister Genette, Shambaugh librarian, who was always eagle-eyed in spotting Pennington materials; to Denise Hughes, who transcribed the tapes and typed much of the original manuscript; to Dr. Nancy Pries for consultation on bibliographic problems; to John and Bertha May Nicholson for their warm hospitality at Westtown and their continued cooperation as representatives of the Pennington family; to Dr. Cecil Pearson for his encouragement and special insights; and to Tina Woodward for her work with and typing the final manuscript.

Preface

THE BIOGRAPHY is a compelling task for anyone whose satisfactions are·bound up with a particular set of activities: relentless pursuit of illusive facts; a skeptical bias that always seeks one more ray of light before venturing a conclusion; a sense of fairness in the face of the bleakest discoveries; and a love for man that invests his work with humility before the sacredness of human life. The biography is also an enormous task when selecting representative data that will fairly picture a life. For example, Levi T. Pennington lived a century less four months. Throughout his life he was active in the many interests of Friends (Quakers): education, the ministry, fundraising, evangelism, temperance, peace, war relief, writing, and politics. In these pursuits he gave hundreds of addresses and sermons, many of which are preserved in manuscripts and notes. In addition he wrote hundreds of reports to official bodies, news stories, articles, fiction, more than three volumes of poetry, an autobiography, and diaries. Always a compulsive writer, he left behind three book-length unpublished manuscripts, and more than 100,000 letters. In order to evaluate his life, a biographer must sift through these thousands of pages plus hundreds of additional pages of writing about him in other correspondence, reports carried in the press, memories of his family, friends, and his antagonists.

Even with this great quantity of information many complexities of his life remain unexplained. What then is the truth about a life? Everyone perceives the events he observes from the vantage point of his own biases. Herein lies the biographer's obligation, fairness to the reader by revealing personal bias, but so deftly that the reader is left free to struggle with his own interpretation of the subject's actions and words. This accounts in part for the inclusion of so many letters and other writing selections.

This biography is critical in the sense that it is evaluative. It is a report on a significant man's life and achievements, written to preserve the subject's perceptions of himself and weighed against the evaluations made by his associates, peers, disinterested observers, and at times by those unfriendly toward him. When opinion on an event in life is contradictory and remains irreconcilable from dependable records, in fairness only the differing views can be presented; they are the truth in its broadest sense.

Pitfalls always await the biographer. How does one get at the truth? Letters and addresses reveal the writer, but there is always the possibility that some facets of the personality will be hidden by the selection of letters retained. Not all of a subject's thoughts are recorded in notes, in diaries, or even letters, but it seems safe to assume that from such primary evidence as personally written letters to intimate friends and family it is possible to construct a dependable picture of a life.

This biography is both selective and limited. It has been researched in an attempt to answer some questions: What were Pennington's ideas? His major concerns? What compelled him to remain in a small college amid frequent misunderstanding and criticism? Why was he such a popular speaker? Why did he give his full energy to fight for unpopular causes? Why was he willing to experience the discomfort of misunderstanding from his own church group? What is the significance of his life? Special attention is given to Pennington the writer. This is not a life story in any traditional sense; rather it is a story of a man's ideas and how he expressed them, for he enriched the world through the art of his language, both spoken and written.

THE FAMILY OF
LEVI T.
and
BERTHA MAY (WATERS)
PENNINGTON

Mary Esther Pennington   b. June 6, 1899
  Married Cecil Pearson   d. October 25, 1976

  Bertha May Pearson   b. November 10, 1926
    Married John Nicholson

    John Talbot Nicholson
    James Anthony Nicholson
    David Parker Nicholson

  Esther Mary Pearson   b. June 19, 1903
    Married Roy Simon

    Alan Charles Simon
    Carol Anne Simon
    Lynn Esther Simon
    Jeanne Louise Simon

Bertha May Pennington   b. June 28, 1903
  Married Leon Pulsifer

Matrix
and
Milieu
1875-1910

In one of Napoleon's famous battles, his forces were being cut to pieces and he ordered his drummer boy to beat a retreat. 'Sire', said the lad, 'I do not know how to beat a retreat. But I can beat a charge. Sire I can beat a charge that will raise the dead!' He beat the charge, the Flower of France responded, and the victory was won. The Prohibitionists do not know how to beat a retreat. But they are beating a charge. Everywhere you can hear the long roll. O, patriots of America, fall in Fall in!

WITH THESE WORDS Levi T. Pennington closed his oration, "The New Patriotism," by winning the Indiana Prohibition Oratorical Contest, March 7, 1908. He was representing Earlham College in competition against five orators from other colleges and universities within the state. This was not his most noteworthy win; it was his first major triumph in intercollegiate oratory. After placing first in the Eastern Interstate division he won second place honors in the Grand National competition at Columbus, Ohio, July 14, of the same year. Two years later he was awarded first place in the Interstate Oratorical Contest sponsored by the Oratorical Society with his oration, "The Evolution of World Peace."

The significance of this activity and recognition was not in the winning of contests, but in the development of a style of public address that in part prepared him for the life of a public figure and popular speaker. Its significance goes beyond style, because his fight for prohibition and for peace together with his attack on

1

human ignorance comprised major crusades and causes for which he became a lifelong champion. His weapon was words—strong, provocative, skillfully used by an imaginative and active mind.

The part which oratorical studies contributed to liberal studies in the last part of the nineteenth and early twentieth century has been largely forgotten. But it served to integrate the liberal arts in which the study of society and moral issues was bound up with logic, composition, psychology, and public address. The oratorical contests were filled with entertainment, drama, suspense, and showmanship while emulating the best of the scholastic mind. William Jennings Bryan had not yet been forgotten, nor the Lincoln-Douglas debates; the American dream was fought for, challenged, and clarified through the appeal to a live audience.

The modern who looks back at an evening spent with a barren stage with a curved line containing six chairs for contestants, and little else for decoration can hardly enter into its excitement. The contestants wearing dark suits with high, wing tip collars and four-in-hand ties stiffly taking their places on stage before a piano duet opened the program seems far too rigid to an informal, individualized generation. After three orations a soloist would emerge to change the pace and rest the tensely listening audience, then three more orations followed by an additional group of solos while the judges carefully tallied their long judging sheets and final scores for determining winners.[1] Then the final, hushed audience listening to every syllable of the judges' decision.

Pictures of these events carry only the form, they cannot convey the interest in the only resource which the world had known up to that time of influencing the world beside the printed page—the human voice. Even at its worst, oratory did not drop to the level of artificiality of motion pictures, radio, and television with their sound men, trick photography, and laugh tracks.

However, its besetting faults finally brought about the end of the oratorical era as its practitioners began falling into idly conventional and stereotyped expression. Coupled with this element of insincerity was an overdependence upon cleverness and a preoccupation with tricks, vogues, and mannerisms which placed an emphasis upon the "dress" rather than upon the thought. Just as the artificiality of euphuistic writing brought about its rejection in the sixteenth century after its initial contribution to the development of the artful English prose of Shakespearian England and the era of the King James Bible, so oratory ceased to exert a healthy influence upon educational experience. The erosion of the valid, thoughtful oration into an "art-for-art's sake" form had not yet taken place during the Pennington years at Earlham.

Three years in oratorical studies for a man in his early thirties who already had experience as a journalist, teacher, and minister provided a matrix for the final stage of his developing style as speaker, writer, and preacher. It is a false dichotomy to think of form and content as separable elements. They are one, for a man's style or form is part of the content of his thinking. The more artful the thinker, speaker, writer, the more tightly integrated the two become. Because of this, Levi Pennington's ideas, his thoughts, and his positions can never be made known fully and accurately except in his own words; his style cannot be paraphrased.

This judgment suggests that something of his style evidently was part of the mental equipment he brought with him to Earlham. But because his earliest written addresses and sermons that can be accurately dated are from the 1908 era, pre- and post-college work cannot be compared for determining the extent college training resulted in stylistic changes. His manuscripts during and following the Earlham years conform to the thought development to which he gave detailed attention in his class notes. If his success in oratorical contests is an adequate criterion for measuring development, it is safe to infer that his progress was rapid. It is probable that he first entered a collegiate contest December 11, 1907, at Earlham with an oration, "Problem of the American City." He did not place. A few months later, in the spring contest of 1908, he was demonstrably successful and remained so throughout his undergraduate career.

What is known of Levi Pennington's early life emerges from his own recollections. Occasional, general information is included in statements from the period of his late twenties and early thirties, but the predominant recollections are from his later years which were published in his *Rambling Recollections of Ninety Happy Years* (1967). His narrative need not be repeated here, but the essential facts of his early life are germane to establishing the character of his early environment, the milieu which influenced his life direction at an early age. From it, his major concerns seized him with such strength that they held him without compromise

during his century of life. Of his family background he wrote to
Errol Elliott, author of *Quaker Profiles* (1972), concerning his
ancestors and life:

> Again let me say that, I am not a genealogist, and I have never done
> research back of my great-great-grandfather. But here is my
> pedigree, as given me by those who are genealogists—they admit it;
> you don't have to prove it.
>
> Robert Pennington. (1550-?)
> Isaac Pennington. (1587-?)
> Isaac Pennington. (1616-1679)
> William Pennington. (1667-?)
> Daniel Pennington, Sr. (1694-1776)
> Daniel Pennington, Jr. (1739-1810)
> Josiah Pennington. (1780-1850)
> Levi T. Pennington. (1812-1896)
> Josiah Pennington. (1842-1928)
> Levi T. Pennington. (1875-   )
>
> I have the names of all the children of these in my direct line of
> ancestors. And I have much information about others in my line of
> both paternal and maternal ancestors. My father's mother was
> Emma Parker, of a notable family of Quakers. My mother was a
> daughter of Joshua and Hanna Cook, and on that side of the family
> there were Cooks and Fernases and Williamses—at my worst I
> could only have been a bad specimen of a good breed.
>
> I was born in a log cabin on David Hadley's farm near Amo, In-
> diana, August 29, 1875. I was sixth in a family of ten children, five
> boys and five girls.[2]

At age eight he entered an ungraded school in the Coffield
School District of Northern Michigan. Four years later he was
registered in the seventh grade in Traverse City, Michigan, in the
last term of the school year, yet completed the grades before his
thirteenth birthday. This became the pattern for most of his formal education: crowding full years of school work into half years
in an era when school terms were only six or seven months at best.
About the time he finished the grades his parents moved thirty-five
miles to Manton, where his father became pastor of the Friends
meeting. Levi remained in Traverse City to attend high school by
living with an older, married brother. To earn money for high
school he worked at a wide variety of odd jobs; however, the scar-
city of even this meager livelihood failed to provide the necessary

money, so at Christmas time and "broke" in his junior year he moved home to his parents at Manton.

This transition ushered in a seriousness to his education in which he was compelled to study for the first time since beginning school. The challenge came about in this way. After a great deal of consultation regarding his transfer, the Manton High School administration placed him in the senior class. But in order to move ahead in it he enrolled for seven subjects; these were completed in two twelve-week terms between Christmas and the end of the school year in June.

His certificate of standing reads:

Manton
Union - Schools
L.N. Tupper, Supt.

Manton, Mich., June 28, 1882

To whom it may concern:

This is to certify the Levi Pennington who has graduated from the Manton High School, is entitled to the following standings, those not appearing having been credited from the Traverse City High School:

Book-keeping	%
Algebra	97 "
History, Gen.	94 "
Geometry, plane	96 "
Rhetoric	99 "
Physics	96 "
Eng. Lit.	97 "
Deportment	Good

(Signed), L.N. Tupper[3]

At this juncture he interrupted the four-year high school course for a year and a half to teach at Roundtop, near Maple City, before returning to complete his diploma and three additional years of teaching previous to becoming head of the Rogers City school. At Christmastime, probably in his fourth year of teaching (1898), he rather abruptly left his school to accept a position of city circulation manager for the *Daily Eagle* in Traverse City. Although not hired as a news writer, he apparently devoted more time to news than to circulation, which erupted in his leaving the paper, "with the unanimous concent of his boss."

After only a few months with an insurance firm, he became a reporter for the rival paper in Traverse City, the *Grand Traverse Herald*, then its city editor, and news editor in fact.

Even though teaching and journalism were his vocation in these early adult years, these activities did not comprise his only interest. During this period he was married to Bertha May Waters (1898) and his two daughters, Mary Esther and Bertha May, were born. It is highly significant that he was also very active in the Friends meeting by serving as superintendent of the Sunday school, president of the Christian Endeavor Society, president of the District Christian Endeavor Union, and speaking frequently in other churches.

The first tragedy of his life occurred with the death of his wife Bertha May (1903). His great love for her, the tragic, overwhelming sense of loss, and blackness of his days as he moved home so his mother could care for his daughters wrenched a sonnet from him which years later he used in one volume of his poetry, *All Kinds of Weather*. This sonnet bore the simple title, "To B.M.W."

When, in the dusk of evening, o'er my soul,
  Like the dull glow that lights the dimming west
  Comes the remembrance of that hour most blest

When my lone-wandering spirit found its goal
In thy dear heart, and of its love the whole
  Rich treasure offered, finding perfect rest
  In sweet fulfillment of thy love confessed
My heart rejoices—then the church bells toll.
  The light dies in my spirit as the glow
  Fades from the distant sky, for thou art gone.

A little taste of heaven here below,
Then night which ever since has darker grown.
  God called thee home, Although I loved thee so;
  God called thee home, and I am left alone.

These fourteen lines embrace the sorrow of a strong man who was bowed by the inexplicable mystery of life, and it speaks still to the man or woman who has suffered a great and deep hurt.

Something of Levi's reputation within the church can be ascertained from an opening that came to him during this period to enter the ministry. At that time, in many Friends circles, young people did not express a desire to serve the church too openly;

rather if the gifts were present in a life and the young person suitable for such a calling, it would be recognized by the elders, who in turn would give both the invitation to serve and the proper guidance. It was simply a way of believing that if the "light" has come to the young person for such a calling, its validity can be attested to by mature members of the society who too will have sensed a "leading" in this direction. They in turn expressed their concerns to the young person and thus his or her calling received both recognition and openings for service.

It was from within this tradition that Levi received the following letter which opened the way for him to enter Christian service full time. This highly significant letter may have been the keystone which brought him into a long life of leadership and influence, and it came to him in a moment in his life in which he could be receptive to the call.

Greenfield, Ind. Oct. 7, 1903

Levi Pennington
Traverse City Michigan

Dear Friend

At our late 'Yearly Meeting' I saw our Yearly Meeting Supt. (J.O. Binford) and also Henry McKinley and on enquiring of each of them in regard to some one to come amongst us as a pastor for two meetings I was recommended to write to thee and see how thee felt about leaving home and home surroundings and taking a charge as pastor for our two meetings in the limits of Walnut Ridge Quarterly Meeting.

Henry McKinley expressed himself as feeling very anxious to see thee have a place and felt very sure that thee would suit us and that we would be pleased with thy work should thee conclude to come this way.

Should thee conclude to come, please state the conditions and terms on which thee could come.

Please answer soon

Very respectfully

J.J. Beeson
Greenfield, Ind.
R.R. No. 3[4]

In order to accept this call and take up his duties as a pastor it was necessary for him to move to Carthage, Indiana, thus leaving his two daughters in his mother's care. Following this move most of his correspondence with his mother was concerned with the girls, especially because Bertha May's health was always a matter of concern during her baby years. She was born to a mother who was very ill, and a two and one-half pound baby without modern hospital care had a hard fight to progress through winter colds and childhood disease. Inseparably bound to this relationship was his growing interest in Bertha May's closest friend, who had helped to care for her during her last illness. It was a delicate matter for a young pastor to develop a romantic interest soon after the loss of his wife to whom he was devoted and whose honor he wished to preserve.

This kind of relationship although prudently developed can be misunderstood in conservative circles. It is no wonder then that some gossip attended his special attention to Rebecca Kidd, but that both Levi and "Becca" were not only aware of it, but found it amusing is indicated by an excerpt from one of her letters to him from Onaway, Michigan, October 2, 1904:

. . . I wish I could know how Baby Mary is this afternoon. I hope that she is better. I wish that you could be there with her. You might not be able to help much but you would feel better.

The 'news' has reached Onaway—not the 'latest edition' but the first 'copy', issued by Rev. Henry McKinley, cousin of the late President, at the Bible Institute in Richmond Aug. 1904. Becca Kidd and Levi T. Pennington are soon to be married.

. . . There is considerable curiosity manifested in regard to my prospects for the winter, which affords me not a little amusement sometimes and again makes me think 'a few.'

The other day I was speaking to Mrs. Stanley about mother's trip west and she surprised me with the remark 'and where does thee expect to go? To some Indiana town near where Levi is?'

I simply ignored the question and *looked* something like this at her, 'I wish people who have such a super abundance of good breeding and refinement could exhibit a little of it occasionally.'

Queer old world this.

That latest report rings in my ears yet. The 'romance of former years', the 'interesting testimony', and the 'larger numbers of letters' etc. nearly convulse me occasionally. I wakened myself this morning laughing at something I had been dreaming. I guess it must have been that.[5]

It must not be thought by the tone of this letter that they were without concern for the opinion of others. Both were utterly sincere in attempting to discover the right course of action for them in regard to marriage. The Pennington family, especially Levi's mother through her letters, gave continued support to his growing love for Rebecca. In a letter written to Levi only a few days before Mary entered senior kindergarten she spoke of her concern for him and her love for 'Becca':

. . . I must answer thy good long letter, thee must not brag on my letter to thee so much as I will get *puffed up*. Glad they do thee so much good, thy letters are a bright spot to us, we are so eager to get them and to know thee is so happy in thy work. While I think about it, can Sam and Hannah have thy couch while she is sick for him to sleep on. She says she will get something to cover it . . . . When thee goes to Indianapolis hope thee can stay a week and rest. I am afraid thee will break down, we need thy letter to cousin Co White. He said I will have to write him, tell that he is going to break down that is the reason one of them thought, 'I wish thee had a good wife to be with thee and help to keep thee from taking on so much.' But if thee was married thee would have to leave off so much and help take care of children and wife for she would have to stay at home so much thee would have to spend all the time thee could with her. . . . I wish we could have been together more. I know we would both have enjoyed it, but I could do without if thee and Rebecca could be together. I knew you could talk better than you could write. . . . Yes Levi I know thee loved Bertha and she knew it too for she said so often to me, 'Poor Levi he will be so lonesome without me. Do everything you can to keep him from thinking about me being gone.' She knew and believed in thee all ways and was proud of thee, would brag about thee to me so much.

. . . I do not think thee is getting tough but is as pure as anyone could be. Levi thy [quotation] from Rebecca's letter was very sound and sensible. Oh she is just fine I think and always did love her, so glad she is the only one thee thinks of more than any one else for a wife. I think she will be all that a wife could be, she must love thee with all her heart to take thee and children and be a wife and mother to them. I believe she will be both.[6]

Throughout these years of activity Pennington sought to improve his education by exploring means for making it possible. Wheaton College (N.Y.) awarded him a Prize Scholarship Certificate for two years' tuition (except for music, business, or art). Certificate number 509 dated September 29, 1896, was a Composition Award in the amount of $55. Even with this assistance he apparently was not able to attend. However, he enrolled in correspondence study in the following years as attested to by a certificate from The American Institute of Sacred Literature in Chicago dated November 1906.

Levi wrote many short stories and several articles with at least a hope for their publication during the years just prior to and just after attending Earlham. It is difficult to establish the beginning of this writing activity, but his occasional use of letterhead paper from the *Grand Traverse Herald* provided a basis for believing that he was writing at least by the time he was with the paper. From both identifiable publication dates and from diary entries it is clear that he was spending a great deal of time writing by 1908. In 1912 he made constant references in his letters to Rebecca that he was not finding time for his writing while on his trips. By this time he was so heavily involved in travel, while raising endowment funds for Pacific College as an added weight to teaching and administration, that the writing of short stories was apparently laid aside, until about 1920.

During this early period he kept a manuscript list in which he recorded the title of his manuscripts, the publications where they were sent, fate (published or rejected), and the amount of money received for their sale. This record book does not give the dates for each story, but judging from publication dates this activity belongs to the period 1900-1912. As an example, the story, "Old Muskie, the Rogue," appeared in *The Youth's Companion*, of September 30, 1909. Other stories and a few articles appeared in *Ram's Horn, The Voice, Christian Endeavor World, American Boy*, and *Collier's*. These were the publications most favorable to his writing, for in them he published a number of his stories. His record book lists thirty-one different writing efforts, mostly stories ranging from seven to more than fifteen pages, of which thirteen were published; several were published more than once.[7] In his private papers belonging to this early period there are also a number of additional stories and articles in manuscript not listed in his book, making a total of about forty short stories and a half dozen articles.

These short stories fall into the general classification of escape fiction, for they contain a strong story line interest rather than developing tightly integrated elements of the image or symbol that is characteristic of interpretative fiction. This statement is not to be construed as a negative evaluation of escape fiction; it is simply an attempt to classify his writing in order to identify more accurately the interests of the man behind this creativity. For an unknown writer to submit unsolicited manuscripts to periodicals and have almost half accepted, many of which were given more than one publication, is a considerable accomplishment. It testifies to an understanding of fiction that publishers sought and that the American people wanted to read. It testifies also to a developing skill in handling character development, plot structure, and creating scenes. A contemporary reader of interpretative fiction might complain of the thinness of his occasional injection of a moral interest in some stories, or of the difficulty of defining the point of view of the narrator in others. Occasionally a story contains a strong autobiographical element, whether actual or fiction, which tends to obscure the actual point of view from which the story should be read. Technically, the relationship of writer to the main character needs clarification in some of his stories.

Pennington was a storyteller throughout his life. His addresses and sermons as well as his letters were full of stories. His friends knew him as a master storyteller who could match a story to the situation. And his dependence upon a story to carry the punch lines of his addresses, and in some cases the major emphasis of an address, shows him as being strongly imbued with the same spirit as Lloyd Douglas, who developed as a storyteller in his sermons, finally moving completely to the novel as his medium of expression. Levi did not move away from the sermon as did Douglas, but there is little doubt but that his long practice of writing stories contributed greatly to his later skill in handling character and story line to provide windows into his points in an address. His consummate skill in integrating story to message goes beyond skillful and economical narration, for he gave the precise shape to his story illustrations that made them unusually effective. They were not intrusions into an address, but were integrated both in tone and substance into the material of the address. It would be misdirected adulation to evaluate these early short stories as significant contributions to literature. However, this large investment of energy made its contribution to Pennington's life even though indirectly, for it served as a matrix for molding his style, enabling him to attain an unusual level of effectiveness as a storyteller. As his mother told him in her letter, perhaps he was a better talker than a writer, at least in this period of his life.

These weltering influences provided the milieu from which Levi Pennington emerged to become a student at Earlham College. His huge strong frame, his physical strength, his dedication of total energy to all tasks and responsibilities, and his indomitable ambition drove him to near superhuman commitments. In an evaluative examination of Pennington's life, his Earlham years must be credited with lifting him to a new level of possibility. It is no discredit to his early years to suggest his explorations of vocation did not establish him on a path toward achievement commensurate with his abilities and ambitions. Each experience, whether in journalism, teaching, or in preaching, became an important influence within the forces which converged upon him to develop maturity and a commitment to serve the Quaker Church.

Thus with two years of pastoral experience at the Wabash Friends Church, during which a new church was built, and more significantly with Rebecca now his wife and mother to the girls, he accepted the call to Knightstown with permission to enroll at Earlham College some forty miles away. He now embarked upon one of the most strenuous periods of his life. To reflect upon this period is to perceive a man who was seizing an opportunity which must be embraced whatever the sacrifice of his own comfort. For two years he carried on the work of the church, yet commuted by train to Earlham early Monday mornings remaining there until Friday afternoon while carrying more than a twenty credit-hour load. Weekends were given totally to the church and to his family. After two years he moved his family to a church in Richmond, which he served while completing his degree in only three academic years rather than four.

These three years and their impress upon him can be called a matrix, for they gave a defined form and style to a life that was still pliable and responsive to discipline and training. Here he was confirmed in his talents, he became known to a wide area of people, he developed friendships that were to remain throughout his life, and he was now prepared for a wider sphere of influence and leadership.

What was his experience and what were his accomplishments at Earlham that so signally and dramatically set Levi Pennington upon a whole new chartered course of life and service? Some insight into answers to these questions can be gained by examining comments about him from the *Earlhamite,* the college publication which covered student activities during the course of the school year. Another source of information can be derived from comments from his schoolmates after, and sometimes long after, graduation. Yet another source is from his own evaluation of the Earlham experience.

Although student publications are not always a valid source of judgment, comments made in them of graduates at least offer a picture of their activities. Less valid are the predictions made for the future of graduates, but in Pennington's senior writeup no prediction was made, although it did contain a listing of activities and successes:

> A.B. Biblical. Thesis-The Messianism of Paul. Y.M.C.A. (1) (3); Oratorical (1) (3); Second Place in National Prohibition Oratorical Contest (1); First Place in State, Interstate, and National Peace Contests (3); First Place State Oratorical Contest (4); First Place Interstate Oratorical Contest (4); Debating Team (1) (3); Member Student Council (3); Track "E" (1) (3); *Sargasso* Staff, '09; Winner of Haverford Scholarship (4).

The following writeup seems significant as an example of student evaluation:

> Pennington's gift of gab and ability as an extempore speaker has been well recognized at mass meetings, contests and many other places. He has been known to tell jokes, has won the highest honors in oratory, debate (?), scholarship and athletics. He is able to turn out more work than any man in school. He is not merely a star, but a whole constellation with a comet thrown in.[8]

Literary efforts which had preceded Earlham days continued while carrying heavy course loads, participation in extracurricular activities, and serving as a Friends pastor. Some of his writing appeared in the *Earlhamite.* It seems only natural that prize-winning orations would appear, so that his oration, "The Evolution of World Peace," was published in the student paper, May 22, 1909. However, some of his fiction also received publication in the same journal. "Mickey McGann," written in dialectic, was published in the issue for June 17, 1910, and "Football and the Faculty" appeared March 25, 1911. His stories of these, his college years, did not take on a sophistication that one might expect of someone studying literature and philosophy in that he did not turn to writing about higher social classes with complex problems. He continued to picture ordinary people with ordinary speech involved with their preoccupations, whether these were in sports or in religion. The significance of this tendency can only be appreciated in the perspective of his entire life. Throughout his career as a public speaker whether before a state bar association, before a state education meeting, or an address for a state organization of newspaper editors, he used illustrations that came from the life of common people whom he knew best. If one can take a cue from the fact that he gave both formal addresses and informal ones, each with a carefully controlled tone that was appropriate for the situation, it must be concluded that he consciously developed a style in which the homey story was frequently used. This assumes that he knew and was in control of his situation, and that homey incidents were told because he wanted to relate to the common roots which he shared with most of his audiences. Stated in another way, he did not draw upon this kind of anecdote without full awareness of what he was doing; it was a conscious part of his style.

Perhaps his athletic attainments at Earlham did not have lifelong significance, yet his performance in field events demonstrates the broad areas of his abilities. He was always interested in sports of all kinds whether football, track and field, or the individualized sport of fishing. Later, while a college president, he used his influence in attempting to improve the moral quality of intercollegiate sports in the state of Oregon, although his high ideal for sportsmanship was not always shared by surrounding institutions. The Spring Athletic Issue of the *Earlhamite*, issued June 5, 1909, records that Levi was a member of the track team by participating in the shot put, hammer throw, and discus. He broke the discus record at the college during that spring.

An example of his willingness if not eagerness to profit from his educational experience is found by examining an address which he read at the Bible Institute held at Earlham College, "Eighth Month, 1909," entitled, "The Quakerism of the Future, A Problem in Synthesis." The organization of his address was founded upon Hegel's law of progress, which emphasized "thesis, antithesis, and synthesis," a central core of the oration which he applied to the Christian church in general and to the Quaker movement in particular to explain its periods of growth and decline. In looking toward the work of the Quakers for the twentieth century he advocated a new unity of Friends, a synthesis of two temperaments within the church, the intellectual and the emotional:

> The intellectuals alone would have a church that would make polar explorations unnecessary for all time. They would move us all to Boston and freeze us all to death. The emotionalists, without some leaven of conservatism, would have us all withered bye and bye in the heat of the intense feeling, or blow us up in some volcanic eruption of hysterical emotionalism. Seriously, a church cannot be made and maintained by either element alone, for it has been tried. The problem of Quakerism in the coming generation is the combination of these two elements, these widely differing camps, into one united force for the conquest of that part of the world assigned to us.[9]

He then demonstrated methods by which the two attitudes could and must be united for building a strong church. This paper could be read as a working model of oratory as he was studying it in the classroom and in such textbooks as *The Rhetoric of Oratory*, by Shurter, a text which he used in his course in Oratorical Analysis. The address follows two distinct organizations integrated into a single unity, first an overall "feeling movement" which correlates with the "thought movement" in the introduction, body, and closing. The feeling movement in the introduction begins with an attention-building device by preparing the audience for possible disagreement with his subject, but with assurances of his seriousness in treating a highly important topic. The thought division within the introduction cradles the thesis that unity is both possible and necessary.

In the body of the address, the feeling element is reinforced by specific imagery and concreteness as he refers to other religious groups and their respective problems, and moves toward climax with a final clear statement of the desirability of obtaining a solution; this is correlated in the thought organization by the antithesis, in which the concrete applications are made to strengthen the otherwise abstraction of the problem. Finally, the conclusion moves through an appeal to the audience for action by stressing obligation, another climax, and a final appeal to volition with an intensity of feeling intended to bring about positive responses to his call for action:

> The church is advancing against the forces of iniquity with solid front. Breaches have been closed, differences healed, our problems in synthesis solved, and the prayer of Jesus more nearly answered than ever before among us, "that they all might be one."

The thought movement of this closing portion of the address is the final urging of his solution (unity), as the burden of his call for synthesis.

It is perhaps impossible to determine if the college experience directed Pennington to new topics for his sermons and addresses. A number of outlines for talks and sermons are preserved in his notebooks from both the pre- and post-Earlham years, and the biblical themes of redemption, sonship, and justice run throughout both periods. It must be assumed that his orations which centered in Peace and Prohibition represented his moral conviction that war was unnecessary, and that alcohol was a form of enslavement not to be tolerated, for these two topics constituted major emphases for the remainder of his life. However, it must also be recognized that oration topics were required to conform to a rigid criterion. Their subject must contain a social problem, and one that is solvable, i.e., be subject to human correction. It must be a living problem, one that demands change now. Problems such as War, Peace, Prohibition, Patriotism, Liberty, and Problems of the American City were featured in nearly all of the oratorical contests. His interests in these subjects appear to have been as keen before enrolling in Earlham in 1908 as they were following his graduation three years later.

These topics were nearly all among the vital concern of Friends, and it may be that his own personal conviction in arguing for peace or for equality was partially responsible for the forcefulness of his presentations. Regardless of that, this kind of topic captivated him; they were not merely subjects suitable for orations. Otherwise his subjects would have changed following college instead of remaining a part of his lifelong argument. However, as he later wrote, the Earlham College experience broadened these subjects to include other human faults which he believed were correctable, which he challenged with the persuasiveness developed in college.

Indulging in this kind of conclusion regarding the college influence upon his life must be recognized as somewhat speculative. Although many of his topics are recorded in notes remaining from his earliest days of speaking and preaching and although dozens of manuscripts remain from 1911 until his death in 1975, some change in his presentations would be expected from experience and maturity if college training were not involved. The comparison of earlier with later talks as a means of assessing college training leaves too many factors which need to be considered before drawing very broad generalizations. It is safe to conclude that his alumni oration to the Traverse City High School in 1895, one year after his graduation, called "Life Thoughts," is little more than a collection of post-high school considerations of fame interspersed with quotations from well-known poems. In substance, in symmetry of form and movement, and in the careful crafting of detail and emotion it bears little resemblance to his college orations, and to his later addresses.

Pennington remained a loyal alumnus of Earlham throughout his life. He maintained continuous contact with classmates, with the president and other officers in the college. His correspondence includes letters both to and from each of the presidents of the college throughout his life. Frequently he visited the college; he was honored for giving continuously for twenty-five years. And the college frequently honored him with pictures and writeups about his activities in the *Earlhamite.* Earlham honored him with an honorary Doctor of Laws, June 5, 1960.

The earliest appraisal of his Earlham experience is contained in a letter written in response to one who had inquired of him concerning the "spiritual" life of the college. In his handwritten draft of the letter he wrote in part:

Dear Friend:

Your letter of the 20th is before me. I doubt the value of my reply to your inquiries for several reasons. In the first place, I was much more mature when I entered Earlham than are most students both in years and in Christian experience, as I did not get to college until I was more than 31 years of age, and I had already been an active pastor for years. In the second place, there has been so great a change in the teaching force since I was a student that what was true at that time might not be true today. There has been a change in the presidency, in the whole biblical teaching force, and in many other teaching positions. In the third place, since I was an active pastor all the time of my student days at Earlham, the center of my religious life and activities was not in Earlham, but in the meetings I served. I could not be as actively associated as I desired with the religious life of the college, could not attend the meetings on Sunday, and was never appointed to a position in the college Y.M.C.A., as I remember it.

I cannot say that my own religious life was affected by my experiences while at Earlham, being as I have said an active Christian and a minister before I entered college. I was enriched intellectually, in my religious life. My vision was greatly enlarged as to the world's need, and I was deepened in my appreciation of the Christian attitude and especially the positions that are characteristic of Friends.

With the relatively so little chance for close touch with the religious life of the student body, I am less able to answer your second question.

Some students doubtless experienced a weakening of their religious faith as they saw what seemed to them an irreconcilable conflict between science and history on the one hand and their ideas of revelation and faith on the other. I suppose this is an inevitable result where ever higher education shows the inadequacy of the old, either in the world or of mind. It ought to be said, however, that this unsettling process must be far less serious where the teaching is reverently done, as was the case when I was in Earlham.

On the other hand, some students while I was in Earlham found a basis of faith which they had deemed impossible, and were really settled and strengthened in their religious life. In evangelistic meetings among the men, the head of the biblical department preached salvation from sin by faith in Christ Jesus, and men were converted. As to the percentage of those who were helped and those who may have experienced a weakening of their faith, I was not close enough to the student body in its religious life to make an intelligent estimate. I should say that the result was far better than if the students had been in the average college even the average denominational college.

I feel it only fair to say that I was invited to lead in evangelistic meetings for the men of the college, and that these meetings were held last week. I was deeply gratified by the number of men on the faculty who attended these meetings and so far as I could see backed up the evangelistic effort as fully and enthusiastically as could be desired. I was given every opportunity in the special meetings for men, in the chapel services, in the regular Sunday morning meeting and in the Y.M.C.A. meeting. I believe that dozens of young men received definite blessing. In more than 50 personal conferences with students, I found that very many were feeling the pull toward the Christian life, and that comparatively few, as far as I could learn, were confronted with any really serious intellectual problems relating to religion.

Perhaps is is always safe to give the admonition to those who teach that they exercise the greatest care and deepest reverence in dealing with things that have religious bearing. That physician would be culpable who would speak of my mother or even of a disease which affected her in any but the most careful and respectful and dignified way. How much more careful and respectful and dignified, how cautious and reverent should be the teacher's approach to things that have a religious bearing! Even in the realm of history and science, he should feel that he is on holy ground, since all truth is God's truth. And in any teaching that touches religious life and religious teaching, even with the purpose of enlarging the life and correcting the teaching, one should be supremely careful, lest he should offend one of these little ones that believe in Christ. . . .

With the prayer that Earlham may continue in ever increasing measure to advance the interests of the Kingdom of God and of the Society of Friends, I am sincerely your friend,

Class of 1910.[10]

The comments in this letter go beyond a simple evaluation of Earlham, for in it he conveyed a great deal of his philosophy of what the Christian college should be, a perspective he took with him to the presidency of Pacific College.[11] How much of this philosophy he acquired at Earlham cannot be ascertained, but he emerged from his college experience as a strong exponent of evangelical Christianity. His three years there became a focal point to which he always referred. Possibly this in itself stands as the best evidence for believing that Earlham College provided stimulation both intellectual and spiritual to a man mature enough to appreciate the influence of the faculty, and the value of forming lifelong, meaningful friendships. It was the maturation of a young man from a milieu of family and community which had made such an indelible impression upon him that he was converted and persisted in loyalty to the convictions inherent in the concerns of Friends. It was further a matrix which helped to give form and discipline to an eager and responsive mind, and finally it was a time of obtaining a widening vision of service to mankind.

Notes to Chapter I

1. Levi Pennington was accompanied to the State Prohibition Oratorical Contest at Valparaiso, Indiana, March 7, 1908, by Walter R. Miles (Earlham '06), at which he placed first, as is indicated by the judges' markings in a copy preserved by Mr. Miles. A copy of the ballot is given below to illustrate the areas in which evaluations were made. Mr. Miles commented on the ballot, "Pennington and I went to the contest together. It was a stiff contest especially on delivery. Of course there were some disappointed ones as there always are. One De Pauw man said that he thought De Pauw would now be ready to stand bare footed in the snow before Earlham."

MARKINGS OF THE JUDGES

Universities and Colleges	Manuscript - Judges						Delivery - Judges						Total Rank	Place
	TC Trueblood Uni. Mich.		Geo. R. Stuart		H.S. Warner		C.F. Holler South Bend		E.E. Blake		Geo. C. Hood			
1. Indiana Uni.	85	4	92	1	90	3	83	5	65	2	82	5	20	3
2. Valparaiso Uni.	84	5	84	6	81	7	75	8	47½	7	79	6	39	7
3. Earlham College	90	3	92	1	95	1	89	2	67½	1	89	1	9	1
4. Taylor University	92	1	80	7	87	5	90	1	60	3	84	4	21	4
5. DePauw University	91	2	90	3	92	2	85	4	55	4	86	3	18	2
6. Purdue Uni.	82	6	90	3	78	8	78	7	45	8	76	7	39	7
7. Tri-State College	81	7	80	7	85	6	88	3	52½	5	87	2	30	5
8. Ind. Central Uni.	80	8	89	5	88	4	79	6	50	6	74	8	37	6

2. This information supplied by Mr. Pennington appears to have been taken from a broadsheet, "Pedigree of Pennington of Denham . . ., reprinted from a History and Pedigree of the Pennington," compiled by Joseph Foster, 21, Boundry Road, St. John's Wood, London, N.W. (n.d.)
3. Family Papers (FP).
4. (FP). For purposes of uniformity the form of many letters has been modified.
5. (FP).
6. (FP).
7. (FP).
8. Shambaugh Library (SL).
9. (SL).
10. (FP).
11. The name Pacific College was changed to George Fox College in 1949. To be consistent with letters, reports, addresses, and other documents cited in the text, Pacific College will be used in all references to the college prior to the name change, and George Fox College in subsequent references.

CHAPTER
II

The Crucible of Administration

1911-1919

DIARY ENTRIES for June, 1910, record the progress of Levi Pennington toward graduation from Earlham College: June 9, "Exempt from all exams"; June 13, "Got thesis in OK *all* work done"; June 17, "Got my A.B. from Earlham. Afternoon and evening at home. After dinner with Seniors"; June 21, "Most of day working at home. Got offer of presidency of Pacific College."

Despite offers of positions from two Quaker colleges, Pacific College in Oregon and Penn College in Iowa, Levi had already decided to continue as pastor at the South Eighth Street Friends Meeting in Richmond for another year, for he entered in his diary, "Engaged house, 119 So. 13th St., one year at $25 a month."

A good picture of Pennington, the man, emerges from two frequent diary entries during the summer of 1910 following his graduation: fishing and writing. In August he went on a fishing trip, apparently without his family, although his diary does not make this clear. He wrote, "Caught some trout," "Caught fish in Flat River, two bass in the lot." Other days when not fishing during the summer months he entered, "Wrote at home." These entries show two preoccupations which he was forced to sacrifice to duty for much of his life.

The story of how he finally decided to accept a position at Pacific College is not complete. It is a story he almost told, but he stopped short of revealing how he made up his mind. His diary entry of receiving an offer of the presidency of Pacific College in

June is interesting because he did not make an entry regarding the initial offer from Acting President W.J. Reagan dated April 20, 1910, which read:

Newberg, Oregon
April 20, 1910

Mr. Levi Pennington
Richmond, Indiana

Dear Mr. Pennington:

I've been asked by the board to write you concerning a position in Pacific College. I realize that you can do better financially out there, but I doubt whether you can do more good. Last Y.M. they voted to start a Biblical Dept. in the college with a man at the head who could work some in the Y.M.

They pay $600-$700 salaries. I think you could get $700 alright. There is a little town down the R.R. track about 2 miles, where there is a Friends' church. They could pay you $300 with a house. Of course there is a possibility that they will have a pastor before we could get word from you.

In college you would have two Greek classes. Then all students have Scripture once a week & you could work up some other courses.

Out here as in other places Friends are not entirely united. They do however seem willing to unite on you. Allen Jay can tell you about conditions here.

Pres. Kelsey has resigned & I'm doing the work until they find the professors.

May I hear from you at once please,
Sincerely yours,

W.J. Reagan

P.S. I feel sure that in addition to your school work you could get some pastoral work. I think Springbrook people would take you. W.J.R.[1]

It is obvious that some kind of understanding was reached between the college and Levi by the end of the summer that he should come as president, although final arrangements had not yet been completed. The basis for this judgment rests upon his correspondence with the college beginning September 19, 1910, and continuing until his arrival in Newberg, Oregon, the following spring. It should be noted that on the day following that of Reagan's letter, Oliver Weesner also wrote to Pennington from Newberg urging him to consider coming to Pacific College. Weesner had been in Earlham with Pennington, but had already moved to the West Coast to teach mathematics at Pacific College. His letter urged Pennington to come as a Bible teacher for an annual salary between $600-$700. He also mentioned the possibility of Pennington's serving as pastor of the Springbrook Friends Meeting with a house and $300, as had Reagan. Anyone familiar with Newberg and its churches, however, would identify that as the little town about two miles up the railroad tracks without the postscript, for in that period the train was the chief mode of transportation from Newberg into Portland, and the Springbrook station is about two miles east of the college. It can hardly be doubted that Reagan had asked Weesner to write thinking that his influence might be helpful in persuading Levi to move west. A few months later in Reagan's letter of September 19, 1910, the second paragraph opened with a statement which implies that an agreement might have already been reached that Pennington was to become the next president, although the nature of the report the board desired on Pennington remains ambiguous.

Dear Pennington:

A member of the faculty com. asked me to write you concerning a trip out to Pacific C. Our Q.M. comes last of Oct. & a board meeting occurs at that time. The Com. wants a report concerning you, at that meeting.

Would you consider the presidency for a period of years? Can you visit this place early in the year? About what would you expect financially? Have you any questions to ask concerning the school before you make the trip? I think the board will bear part or all the expenses of the trip. Have you any experience in school work?

I hope the visit may be arranged for soon. Prospects are good for an increased attendance.

May I hear soon. This letter is written at request of faculty com.

Yours,
W.J. Reagan

Letters from Reagan the following spring show plans underway for Pennington's taking over the administration of the college. On March 13, 1911, he wrote as follows, in part:

Dear Pennington:

Your letter came and I'm sending you under separate cover a catalogue with all courses marked down. I think the teachers here this year can manage their courses if the catalogue is to remain unchanged.

. . . Have you any suggestions for changing courses? I'm anxious to help you all I can, but you must remember that these people think of you as Pres. of Pacific College, they do not expect me to decide things with reference to the future.

. . . They are arranging for dedication for commencement. When will you get out here? Do you want catalogues put out before you come? We will work the field hard until Commencement, but there ought to be someone busy all summer. One man thought you ought to come to Yearly Meeting even if you had to go back again at once.

With every best wish,

W.J. Reagan

On April 24 Reagan wrote again to insist that Pennington come as early as possible. He gave some evaluation of the staff who would be carrying part of the load of the college until his arrival, and concluded with inquiries concerning a house which was under consideration for lease. The following day Reagan wrote him again apparently to give an additional incentive for his coming to Newberg by Yearly Meeting time:

Dear Pennington:

I wanted to leave here Sun. night, but we have arranged Educational Session for Mon. June 19. You will be expected to give the address. I feel there will be a decided increase in enrollment next year. I hope people will continue their present attitude toward you.

. . . Have been frosting windows at the new building this P.M. You will be head janitor of the institution as Pres. The head janitor gets to do the extras.

Sincerely,

W.J. Reagan

In another letter (May 8, 1911), Vice-President Reagan discussed the problems encountered with staffing for the following year and asked for Pennington's wishes concerning two staff positions and the proposed salaries. Two items in his letter point out specific concerns that were in his mind with the prospect of a new president coming to assume leadership of the college. In the third paragraph of this letter he stated something of the financial condition of the college, but unless more was written than this, the real financial crisis was not very evident. "I think the $400 is about raised. That building referring to the recently erected Wood-Mar Hall took all the extra, so it's been unusually hard to make ends meet. We are about 3 months behind on salaries here." The closing of his letter expressed concern over the prospect of leaving before the new college president could arrive, something he had mentioned in previous correspondence, "We will leave for Summer School at Chicago as soon as possible. I will be about a week late anyhow. I want to stay till you come if possible. We ought to leave Sat. night."

The first part of another letter dated June 7 conveys further details concerning Pennington's arrival at the college; the last part of the letter discussed arrangements for a house previously proposed for $10 per month rent. This letter opens:

Dear Pennington:

I've not heard from you yet, but I'm informing you of some of our ideas about the school. The faculty seem to think there ought to be four years academy. Also they are inclined to lengthen the Re. period & decrease the no. of credits for graduation.

Each teacher is working on his department & we will send our suggestions soon.

L.A. Wells says you will gain a whole year, by getting out [for] the Y.M. education address. I've suggested that we have dedication & inauguration at the same time, if you will be here.

Levi Pennington took over the presidency of Pacific College with the opening of the fall term, 1911. The situation awaiting him and the staggering load to be undertaken with a tiny college and academy facing some grave problems, if explored only briefly, will show why this first eight-year period of Levi's presidency was a crucible of administrative experience. In these eight years, gains were always lost by reason of circumstances: at times inherent within the position of the college, at other times by virtue of the economy, and at still other times by the shifting opinion and support of Friends who sponsored the college. The final near death blow came in World War I with sharp decreases in students augmented by the unpopularity of a Quaker college which continued to speak for the cause of *peace* in a society which was emotionally charged for war. The miracle of these crucible years, these years between 1911-1919, relentless months and months of stress and fatigue, is that the college was not crushed by the antagonisms of a war period, but was ready for the return of students following the Armistice. Credit for this achievement cannot be given to any one person.

The college which called Pennington to serve as its head was opened as Friends Pacific Academy in 1885 with a student body of nineteen and three faculty members. The success of the academy in that its enrollment reached 130 by 1890, and still the nearest Quaker college for its graduates was Penn College in Iowa, prompted the board to announce the opening of Pacific College in 1891, to strengthen Quaker educational opportunities in the Pacific Northwest. By this time the school was housed in two buildings: Hoover Hall, which had served as the main academy building, and Kanyon Hall (later renamed Minthorn Hall). These buildings situated on a twenty-three acre campus were moved to a new campus, and a gymnasium added during the administration of Thomas Newlin, first president of the college.

Henry Edwin McGrew, the second president, was seated in 1900 and immediately undertook the task of raising money for an endowment as a means of overcoming the deficit financing threatening future hopes for the college. In 1901-1902 he headed a campaign that raised $14,500 to eliminate the accrued debt. In 1905 a proposed campaign to raise an endowment of $50,000 was launched, but not completed because of McGrew's health, which caused his resignation in 1907. The third president inherited many problems from the endowment campaign, but notwithstanding he made a great contribution to the development of the college with his appointment of some competent faculty who were to become long tenured, thereby making enormous contributions to the college. President Kelsey remained only until 1910, but his selection of staff and their subsequent contribution will always be an important chapter in the college history. He was succeeded by an acting president, Professor W.J. Reagan, who remained until the spring of 1911 for the coming of the fourth president, Levi T. Pennington. Perhaps the other significant event during Reagan's acting presidency was the building of the present administration building, Wood-Mar Hall, completed in 1910. The raising of the $30,000 necessary for erecting this badly needed building is one of the great sagas of college history, because of two dedicated ladies, Amanda Woodward and Evangeline Martin, who canvassed the community in their buggy for money to build this historic hall.

Pennington came upon this scene charged with a plethora of responsibilities: heading a new endowment campaign; finding cash for college operations, for cash flow had always been a problem but made more acute because of completing the new Administration Building; seeking recognition as a Standard College by the Department of Education; and developing loyalty within the constituency.

In his first year as president, Pennington reported a student body of forty-one in the college, fifty-one in the academy, and forty-two in the music department. In the spring commencement of 1912, nine students were graduated from the high school and five from the college, an increase over the enrollments of the years just preceding, offering some optimism to the new president. But this was not a trend to be depended upon, for to gain enrollment President Pennington was under pressure to obtain standardization. But the first prerequisite for meeting this standard was the development of a $100,000 endowment fund. Thus he was in a vicious circle.

Early in the school year 1911-12 the Board of Managers took action to launch a drive for obtaining this goal, and thus within his first year as president Levi was thrust into a taxing and frequently frustrating endeavor. In his report to the Yearly Meeting (1912), Board Chairman E.H. Woodward reported this board decision, and further reported that President Pennington had been soliciting funds for the past six months. The new president had come to Pacific College without previous college teaching or administrative experience, without graduate work, and without wide acquaintance in the Northwest, but his crucible was to be thrown immediately into these two closely related but separate problems: raising an endowment, and upgrading the college educational program to make it acceptable to the United States Bureau of Education.

Financial campaigns are always difficult even when opened within a good climate, but this new drive followed by only five years an abortive attempt to raise a $50,000 endowment. In that drive subscriptions were not binding until the total amount was raised; consequently, in its failure, psychological barriers were erected to inhibit a second attempt. One of the significant handicaps which this fund drive posed for Pennington was to commit him to solving a problem not totally of his making, for it remained from the past. In terms of launching a new administration, he was partially absorbed with a continuing problem rather than being able to offer fresh initiative.

How did President Pennington begin his new assignment? Some indication of how he was to proceed is given in his first annual report to the Yearly Meeting in 1912 in which he discussed an initiative toward standardization he had already undertaken:

> The work in both college and academy has been divided into semesters, and the requirements for entrance and graduation have been increased to measure up fully to the requirements of the standard college. One full year has been added to the academy course. Greater liberty is allowed in the choice of subjects in the college, but enough 'required work' is retained in each course to insure that the education shall be well rounded, even with the maximum of specializing that is allowed.[2]

Little did he know this struggle would last for the next thirteen years, but in it he had launched an attack upon what seemed to him a discrimination against a small, struggling college. Not that it was leveled against any particular school, but against any school in like circumstances. Without adequate endowment and approved physical equipment, standardization was out of the question, but without it money for improving facilities was almost impossible to raise. This situation constituted a vicious circle, which he set out to make clear both to the state of Oregon and to the United States Bureau of Education. His attempts to clarify the plight of the college were met by a noncommittal attitude by L.R. Alderman, Superintendent of Public Instruction for the state of Oregon, who would make no commitment stronger than that expressed in the following letter:

February 19, 1912

State of Oregon
Department of Education
Salem

To Whom it may concern:

This is to certify that I am acquainted with the grade of work done by Pacific College, Newberg, Oregon, and I am pleased to say that the work in that institution has always been thorough. Its graduates are making good in whatever calling they have taken up. I know the members of the faculty, and know them to be able, earnest people. The college has beautiful surroundings, and is located in one of the best towns in the state.

Yours very truly,

L.A. Alderman[3]

This is the kind of letter that any college administrator dislikes to receive from an official, for although constituting a kind of pat on the back, it falls short of endorsement.

This letter to President Pennington followed a report which Alderman had received from Kendric C. Babcock, Specialist in Higher Education in the Bureau of Higher Education, and approved by P.P. Claxon, United States Commissioner of Education, dated January 31, 1912. This was a report of an investigation of Oregon colleges and universities with a special section devoted to Pacific College.

The complete text of this special section follows:

Among the principal deficiencies to be overcome by Pacific College before it can be classed as a standard institution are:

1. The requirement of four years of high school work instead of three years for admission.
2. The clear separation of college from preparatory work for students and for at least half of the faculty.
3. A great improvement in the library and laboratories of biology and physics. The present laboratory in chemistry might suffice for good general chemistry and qualitative analysis.
4. An unencumbered endowment of $200,000. The present endowment is offset by debts of nearly the same amount.[4]

By June, Pennington was able to stir up a spirited controversy with the Bureau in Washington. In 1912 colleges were still dealing with the Department of the Interior when seeking accreditation because this department supervised the Bureau of Education, which in turn directed the Division of Higher Education. This layering of interests had to be penetrated in pleading a case for recognition as "Standard." Nevertheless, Oregon's newest college president took pains to point out some of the inconsistencies that were involved when a small college undertook recognition. The following letter from Kendric le Babraell, Specialist in Higher Education in the Division of Higher Education, reveals the attitude and thinking which President Pennington encountered:

President Levi T. Pennington
Newberg, Oregon.

My dear President Pennington:

Much absence from the office has caused a long delay in replying to your letter of May 6th, and you have my apology for the neglect.

You are entirely correct in assuming that Oregon has the right to determine the qualifications of her high school teachers. This she has attempted to do in the law of 1911, and in doing this she has solicited and received the assistance of the United States Bureau of Education. This Bureau, however, does not seek in any way to dictate the standards or the procedure for determining the qualifications of teachers in the State of Oregon. We are completely willing to cooperate in any way possible in improving the standards according to any legal and judicious method.

The saving clause in your first paragraph, from my point of view, is 'that will give him employment.' This would be true in the State of Oregon all the way from the College of Philomath to Reed College or the University of Oregon! It is not fair, however, to say that a man who has sneaked through the college which was next to the weakest, should be compared with a brilliant fellow graduated from the strongest of the non-acceptable institutions of Oregon. I am quite ready to admit that the best student graduating from McMinnville College might be more qualified for teaching in the high school than the poorest graduate entitled to a certificate through the University of Oregon or Stanford University, but that does not prove to my mind that McMinnville or Stanford should be classed together.

The practical question of changing through legislation the present method of standardization in Oregon is not one which I ought to discuss beyond saying that special legislation exempting certain institutions from compliance with present standards would be much less desirable than a frank and regular adoption of a lower general standard which would admit certain institutions now excluded even by the liberal interpretation given to the present law.

In answer to your last question, my judgment is that the variance in enforcement of standards of admission and in content and spirit of the four years course above graduation from high school, especially such parts as fall within the third or fourth collegiate years, would make it undesirable to place the granting of high school teachers' certificates solely upon the formal completion of the eight years course which you mention. The personnel of the faculty, requirements of teaching, mixture of classes, equipment of laboratories, and relations with a constituency should all enter into the determination of standards.

Let me assure you once again of my interest in your problems in Oregon, and of my desire to assist in their solution so far as I am able.

Very truly yours,

Kendric le Babraell
Specialist in Higher Education[5]

Later in his first annual report to Oregon Yearly Meeting Pennington pointed out two anxieties concerning the college:

There are two great needs of the college as it faces the future, and one of these depends upon the other. The first and greatest need is loyalty—the continuance of the loyalty that has brought the college thus far by such sacrifice as can be duplicated in America, and the development of similar loyalty on the part of many who have not yet felt as fully as they should their responsibility for the college and its need for their help.

The other need, and it will be met if the college has the loyal support in the coming days that it should have, is the need for funds. . . . It is hoped that there will be the greatest loyalty in the support of the campaign for $100,000.00 endowment, which the board of managers of the college are seeking to raise by January 1, 1913.[6]

These two needs, pointed out in his first annual report, without doubt represent his analysis of what tasks were to be undertaken, based upon one year of observation of the college from the vantage point of a newcomer who was willing to give himself completely to the challenge ahead. It is hardly surprising that as summer came President Pennington gave a high priority to the proposed endowment drive. This meant that he must look outside of the Northwest for finances to Friends in the East. That was the center of his acquaintance, and thus began a life of frequent trips to the Midwest and East. As an enthusiastic trout fisherman and as a man devoted to his wife and daughters, these arduous days of travel seemed to have pulled him away from the life he would have enjoyed most. A trip East meant as many as five days on a pullman from Portland before beginning the rounds of appointments, both private meetings with those whom he might interest in Pacific college and speaking in many churches from Richmond, Indiana, to Philadelphia or New York.

To most of those who knew Levi Pennington he was outgoing, sociable, and courageous. His ability to meet strangers appeared relaxed and stimulating. His entire manner would have convinced even a doubter that he thrived on travel and public appearances, but there was another side to his personality and nature that was concealed from view.

He was a man who was imaginative, sensitive, and tender, a man for whom long trips away from home were spent in reading, but always interspersed with long letters to Rebecca, at least one letter each day, often two, and not infrequently three. Wherever there was the possibility of posting a letter at the next stop he pulled out his small, ruled tablet and pencil to dash off another few pages of adoration to his "Becca." Because of his eye for countryside, his pleasure associated with lakes and streams, his interest in men, women, and children surrounding him, most of his friends would have expected him to write of these interests, but no! He poured out his affection to the one woman with whom he was in love and shared with her his lonely vigils of travel that took him away from Newberg. He could reveal his own sense of being alone to her, for she understood that beneath his exterior gregariousness there was a small boy's love of home and familiar surroundings. This was Levi Pennington the private man.

A report of this trip through his eyes as he recorded it in his letters to Rebecca conveys a great deal of the man. He expressed his wistful sentimentality as he wished she could be with him to enjoy the friendship of reunion with friends, and especially to share the grandeur of Niagara Falls, the appeal of Coney Island, and the continuing expanse of countryside that unfolded outside of the train windows.

Within these wistful letters he revealed much of his own Victorian sense of how men and women must behave toward each other. This was not the artificial, euphemistic Victorian stance, but rather the strong expression of what was proper as it had been taught to him in his environment.

These letters also occasionally show the ego by which he was capable of comparing himself with others. He often felt that he could chair a difficult meeting better than the one presiding, and as often too true of the able person, his evaluation may have been valid.

From early July until after mid-August President Pennington traveled through Ohio, Indiana, Michigan, into New England and eastern Canada in raising money for the endowment. He wrote to Rebecca on the morning of July 6 as the train neared Chicago that he had been lazy on the trip, writing no stories, reading but little, and thinking only when playing checkers. On this day he had become the car champion. He faced the days ahead with a certain dread of raising money, although he was rested. The night of July 4 he reported sleeping all night without awakening and he broke from his usual habit of writing letters for posting throughout the day, for on the morning of July 5 he began a letter at Cheyenne, Wyoming, but did not finish it until considerably later when the train was in North Platte, Nebraska. His normal habit would have been to write a second letter by the North Platte stop.[7]

Atlantic City, New Jersey
7/11/12

My Darling Wife:-

The convention has been having a cat and mouse time. The permanent chairman, a spendid, good old man, is not big enough in voice, energy or forcefulness, to hold the warring factions in any semblance of order, and . . . who was largely responsible, or rather wholly responsible for my failure to be suggested as permanent chairman by the Oregon delegation, has eaten humble pie in large chunks. He is getting what's coming to him, and it seems awful. He could have had me for permanent chairman if he had so desired. . . .

I do not wish to be an egoist, but dearie, I do know that if I were in the chair, we'd have been farther along in this work. For instance, the rules explicitly state that this is the order in bringing business before the convention: The Motion; the amendment; the substitute; and then no more business 'till this is disposed of. Instead of this, we had a motion, a substitute, an amendment, another amendment, another motion, a motion to refer, a suggested amendment accepted by the committee, etc., and just where we are now it might be difficult for a better man than the chairman . . . to tell us. . . .

. . . Good-night, my own dear love of a wife. If my love at this distance can bless you, there in the blessed home you make for me the blessing of my love is sweetly upon you.

Your very own forever,
Levi

Plymouth to Somewhere or other, Indiana
July 7, 1912, 6 p.m.

My Darling Wife:-

I've had my supper, and now I am going to write a bit to the sweetest, truest little woman in the world, who's mine and whose I am, and glad of it. If I didn't love her with all my heart, maybe I'd not be so enthusiastic. . . .

You'll be glad to know, dearie, that I'm not finding the trip thus far as disagreeable as I feared it would be. It isn't because I do not long for you, for I do, all the time. The things that are unpleasant would be pleasant, many of them, if you could be with me. The pleasant things as it is, would be delightful if you were along. How much it would mean wouldn't it, my sweet? if together we could visit Chicago, Philadelphia, Atlantic City, New York, Niagara Falls, Detroit, Winona Lake, Indiana, Minneapolis, St. Paul, and the Rockies on the Canadian Pacific. Someday, sweetheart, maybe after the girls are both in college or sometime, we are going to take our honeymoon tour. And as I see it now, it will include the Yosemite Valley, the Royal Gorge, Yellowstone Park and Niagara, with New York, the Pacific Ocean, Alaska, and Mexico as possible side trips. You deserve such a trip—and I'm your husband and ought to go along to help take care of you. May I go with you, dearest? . . .

Lovingly always your very own,
Levi

Toronto, Canada
July 16, '12

My Darling Wife:-

. . . And now I feel a good deal like a criminal. What right has a fellow to enjoy what I have seen today without his wife? Niagara Falls and the Gorge, Whirlpool Rapids and the Whirlpool—O, dearie mine, if only *You* could be with me!

Lovingly as ever and for ever,
Levi

Another letter written from Detroit, July 21, 1912, is very long and quite personal, but even a few lines convey his love for Rebecca. He had written to assure her that she was of great worth to him, that in her role as a loving wife she was making possible his contribution as a leader. The letter opens and closes with his assurances of his love for her:

Detroit, Michigan
7/21/12

My Darling Wife:-

It is Sunday morning, and I'm wondering if you are as hungry to see me as I am to see you. Or does the longing to see me grow less as my absence grows longer? To think of my dear wife longing to see me last Sunday, and almost a whole continent between us. . . .

Must go to Sunday School with Hanna. Good bye, dearest. Don't miss me too much, dear—and yet could I wish you to miss me less?

Lovingly, always, dearie,

Levi

Post Script omitted.

Occasionally President Pennington indulged in lighter thoughts as he rode through the countryside. On his return trip on the Canadian Pacific he began a letter in Moose Jaw, Saskatchewan (July 30, 1912), in which he commented:

. . . We passed Portal before I was out of my berth this morning. The Customs Inspector looked at our suitcases, just barely, chalked them with his O.K., and that's all there was to it.

In the past 24 hours we have passed the greatest wheat fields I ever saw in my life. . . . We are now in the country of the snows, as one can see by the frequent snow-fences along the track. The land is rougher here, and it looks as if there were less rain. It is cattle country, and not the rich farming land we saw farther east and south.

The psychological weariness from Herculean efforts to raise a $100,000 endowment for meeting "standardization" criteria can be dramatized by reference to the January 31 (1912) report from Washington, D.C., in which item four called for an endowment of $200,000. President Pennington believed this figure to be a change from earlier criteria, and it can only be conjectured that he was sustained in part with hopes that the Bureau of Education would not require this larger amount, although correspondence with the Bureau in March had not resulted in any modification. This conjecture is also based upon his continued efforts to raise the $100,000 and his connecting it with standardization hopes in letters to friends and to possible contributors. Also he gave no sign that the new criterion was a deterrent during his two trips East in the last half of the year to raise endowment funds. Late in the year Pennington renewed his appeal to Washington. It was met with a firm rejection.

Both trips east resulted in minimal contributions with only weak hopes of securing early, substantial financial assistance. The grimness of the fund-raising realities began to be felt in December at the same time that the Bureau of Education in Washington shattered any last, secret hope of a compromise. Thus the first eighteen months of administration ended in the bleakest outlook that a new president could have imagined. As he faced this situation Levi Pennington demonstrated indomitable courage in the dawning of the year 1913. Like the fabled Phoenix, new hope seemed always to rise from the ashes of apparent defeat. He did not collapse under the burden of discouragement; to the contrary he launched a campaign to raise $200,000 for the endowment, even though six months later he was able to report that only $40,000 of the first goal had been raised.

There is no record that he accepted the New Testament challenge, "no one who puts his hand to the plow and looks back is fit for the kingdom," but this describes his sense of purpose. He had always been a competitor unaccustomed to defeat. Earlier he had given his full energy to football with every expectation of winning. He competed in oratory without hesitation. Even at conferences he managed to participate in events that required the competitive spirit, for only six months before he and Daniel Poling joined forces as a rowing crew and were the rowing winners in a conference at Winona Lake, Indiana. While riding on the train he always sought for a foe to challenge in checkers. In conversation he always strove to outdo others in wit and storytelling. His only thought was to remain at Pacific College, where he nursed a hope and exercised a faith that Quaker education in the Northwest was possible, and that it was worthy of his full strength to transform the dream into reality.

Josiah and Mary Cook Pennington,
parents of Levi T. Pennington.

Levi T. Pennington in his early thirties, circa 1908.

Wedding picture of Levi T. Pennington and Bertha May Waters, June 1, 1898.

Levi and Rebecca Pennington, Mary (back), and Bertha May, circa 1916.

But demonstration of a strong will and courage fails to convey fully the manner of man he was in this period of his life. Perhaps the best way to understand the nature of his Christian outlook and his vision of what a Quaker, Christian college ought to accomplish is to read one of the closing paragraphs in his annual report to Oregon Yearly Meeting in its sessions in June 1913.

> It should go without saying that a school of the character of Pacific College should have its definite end the advancement of the Kingdom of God among men. It should not be forgotten that a general education, without which our children, whatever their calling in life, will be handicapped, can be secured to them under more favorable moral and spiritual environment than other institutions provide, this alone would be worth a tremendous sacrifice on the part of all who are interested in the coming generation. But this is not all that is desirable, and this is not enough for Oregon Yearly Meeting to seek for Pacific College and to expect of the college. The institution ought definitely to advance the cause of the Kingdom. It should not only send out men and women competent to enter business or fit themselves for the professions or take their places on the farm or behind the accounting desk, but it should send them out as Christians to take up these lines of activity in the world's work. In the motto of the college, Christianity and Culture, Christianity is rightfully put first. Nor is even this enough. From Pacific College should go, in ever increasing numbers, those who are to take their places in the special work of the Kingdom, as Ministers, Christian Association workers, Home and Foreign Missionaries and others who shall give their lives in this peculiar way to the definite work of the Kingdom.[8]

The struggles during 1914 were a continuation of those from the preceding year, except for the sense of urgency to complete the endowment-fund drive by the end of the year. This continued as the central issue, a key for unlocking the door to securing more students. Although the enrollment had increased during Pennington's tenure, it continued as a matter of concern because its fluctuations reflected instability. In the 1910-1911 school year the college enrollment was 33, the academy 46. In the following year the college enrollment increased to 41, and the academy to 51, but in 1912-1913 the college experienced a decrease to 35 students while the academy rose to 80. In 1913-1914 the college increased to 40 and held that figure for the following year, but the academy began a steady decline that lasted until 1918-1919. This fluctuation picture appears to justify the judgment of the president of the Board of Managers, E.H. Woodward, who wrote in his annual report to the Yearly Meeting in 1914,

> With the teaching force the college now has, double the number of students that have been attending could be accommodated, with but little added expense. The college needs this added number of students and there are those in the territory that we cover who need what the college has to offer to young people.[9]

President Pennington had been asked by the board to teach during the 1913-1914 school year, which he did even though in so doing the endowment drive suffered. Arrangements were made for him to devote more time to this effort during the summer and autumn of 1914, because as he wrote to a friend November 19, the amount already pledged was endangered if the total were not reached by the end of 1914. The goal was reached by the end of the year although not to the satisfaction of all who had made pledges conditioned upon raising the full $100,000.

The significance of this event can only be understood in the light of how highly it was regarded by many who were not in the Friends movement. Early in January 1915 letters began to pour into Pennington's office congratulating him upon this accomplishment. Timothy Nicholson of Richmond, Indiana; Edwin McGrew, president of Whittier College; Rufus Jones; and L.C. Haworth, general secretary of the YMCA. He also received congratulations from the other college and university presidents within the state of Oregon: Kenneth S. Latourette, president of Reed College; C.J. Bushness, president of Pacific University (Forest Grove); and P.L. Campbell, president of the University of Oregon.

Part of the joy of the accomplishment was erased by Pennington's loss of health in which he was forced to take several weeks away from his office. As the months passed it also became painfully evident that endowment gifts and pledges had cut seriously into the regular gifts to the college which precipitated two years of serious financial crisis. Perhaps the greatest threat to the existence of the college was within the American entry into World War I. The war years, bleak for many colleges, were even more intense in a tiny college daring to insist upon the Quaker stand for peace in the midst of an excited nation not only emotionally charged for supporting the war, but condemning the small element in society which preached peace and urged its young men not to accept draft into uniform.

The early war years in Europe began to strengthen the peace testimony of Oregon Friends, and in this sense prepare for a course of action leading to their leadership roles after the United States entered the war. The Peace Report to Oregon Yearly Meeting in 1916 opened with this statement:

> Our hearts are saddened because of the awful war which has been raging in Europe for twenty-two months, and the countries engaged in the conflict do not yet seem willing to have peace. We are amazed at the long-suffering of our Christ, who said, "Love your enemies, do good to them that hate you."

> In our Yearly Meeting there are some encouraging things to report. Our people are awakened on the subject of peace and are studying it from various angles as we have not done for years. Friends had for some time seemed to lose sight of the great principles of the church. Recently our pastors and others have been speaking on the subject, and much interest is manifested.[10]

This new interest resulted in the writing and endorsement of a resolution by the Yearly Meeting in which it reaffirmed the action of Philadelphia Yearly Meeting in its opposition to war and preparation for war. It further affirmed its opposition to a proposed program for military drill in the public schools, either compulsory or voluntary, and it pledged love and loyalty to the nation by expressing a willingness to make rightful sacrifice in the interest of true patriotism. President Pennington's work was not yet negatively affected by the war; in fact he opened his report to the 1916 Yearly Meeting with a statement of optimism concerning Pacific College, "While the halls of other colleges are deserted, their students having gone to the great war, we have been permitted in peace and comfort to prosecute our work as a college." The financial hardship was intense during this period, but this condition was still the result of the drying up of gifts following the endowment drive. In a short time gifts would become difficult to obtain as a consequence of the war.

But changes became apparent in the 1916-1917 school year which led President Pennington to report to the Yearly Meeting in June, 1917:

During the year that has just closed, and especially during the latter part of it, the shadow of the world war has been over Pacific College, as over every other body of students in the country. As citizens of the United States, now engaged in the great war, we have sought to keep our loyalty on the highest possible plane. As representatives of the Society of Friends we have earnestly desired to be true to the truth for which Friends have stood from the beginning. As representatives of Christianity we have endeavored to preserve the spirit of the Savior of the world, and keep from our hearts all hatred and bitterness. And as an institution preparing for their work the future leaders of the world, we have tried to keep our eyes on the ultimate rather than on the immediate service that can be rendered to our country and to the world. —

This statement became a criterion by which he seemed to make evaluations for making personal and administrative decisions throughout the remainder of the war years and during its aftermath. He was called upon to make decisions regarding curricular changes, especially the teaching of German and training directly supporting military training. The hostility against Germany ran so strong that colleges and public schools were discouraged and in other instances prohibited from teaching classes in German. But Pennington answered objections to the continuing of German courses in Pacific College by declaring that if the United States were to assume its proper role following the war it must have young people able to speak and write German for engaging in reconstruction and relief work in addition to the functions of government. When asked by the superintendent of the nearby Portland, Oregon, public schools why he did not curtail German he answered in hardhitting tones that such action would be too shortsighted for adoption by intelligent citizens who are training young people for future lives of service.

A strong quality of his leadership derived from his vision of the future, for always he refused to be wooed by those who sought to satisfy immediate goals at the expense of ultimate purposes. Frequently he spoke and wrote harshly to those who expected him to compromise his judgment. This alienated many from him even though his correspondence is replete with apology. He was hardhitting in his addresses against what he perceived as evil such as war, tobacco, and alcohol. His frankness carried over into business meetings in which he struggled against what he perceived as shortsighted solutions to large problems, but his motivation was to preserve intelligent action. It was his dedication to this ideal, his strong dedication that made him at times a fierce opponent.

Pennington maintained an active interest in young men who reached draft age by helping them make decisions concerning the kind of service they were to enter, whether alternate service to the military or in uniform. Because young Friends experienced great difficulty in attempting to serve in capacities other than in the military, he devoted a great deal of time and energy in giving them assistance. Many were placed under arrest in military camps, and when this occurred he attempted to reach someone close to them who could go directly to their assistance in securing their rights. Others found constant difficulty in their hospital or other service, and to these he wrote encouraging letters to help them see beyond the unpleasant chores such as caring for victims of the flu. One would have expected him to be sympathetic to those who declined military status, but he was equally helpful to other young men who joined the service. One such exchange of letters will convey more of his insight into the young men, his sympathetic respect for them, his sensitivity, and his own national loyalty than descriptive narrative can relate.

1st Provisional Recruit Squadron
Kellysfield
South San Antonio, Texas
November 3, 1917

Dear Mr. Pennington:

I suppose you are back from the East and know that I have enlisted. I hope you will understand in what light I regard enlisting and that I have no way lowered my standard of religion. I was raised a Methodist and always believed in some of their principles. I've felt that I ought to enlist since last spring and got so I felt ashamed everytime I saw a man in uniform so I decided to enlist in the Aviation Corps if possible so went to Portland to investigate and as the Aviation Corps was open I enlisted and am now here.

Now I want to be a flyer and so want to start the red tape moving. The first step is to secure three recommendations and so I want you to give me one. If you feel like giving me one put in a statement of number of years I've went to college. My Scholarship, Marks, Character etc. If you write me one send it to my folks as soon as possible. It takes two weeks to get an answer from home here and a lot more red tape to go through so I want to get things started as soon as possible.

Now I'll give you a sketch of camp life. We are out in a desert with no civilian homes within miles. This camp holds about 20,000 and extends for miles. Thousands of us sleep in tents. The buildings and tents are grouped around the aviation fields which covers hundreds of acres, the whole camp is level as a floor.

It gets awful cold at night and awful hot in the daytime. The other day it changed from 24° to 84°. We have our own mess kits and are served at a field kitchen and eat sitting on the ground and wash our own dishes. We sleep eight to a tent and must fold our blanket up in the morning. We work or drill between meals. It's so cold we can't hardly eat in the morning and we roast at noon. Airplanes fly westward continuously, their engines roaring. Give my address to the senior class.

Very truly yours,

Sewell O. Newhouse

Pennington's response bears the date of November 10, 1917:

Dear Friend:-

I am gladly sending the letter of recommendation you requested, and I hope that it may be just what you wanted. I could have written more, but this seemed to be about what you desired.

I hope that you have not a wrong impression as to how I would feel when I learned of your enlistment. I knew, of course, of your training, and I could guess what your feelings would be in the matter. I honor a man for doing what seems to him the right thing to do. I have felt, as you know, that a college-bred young man could find a larger service for the country he loves than the one that you have chosen. But I have tried to make it clear that I feel the deepest sense of loyalty to America, and feel that it is the duty of every one of us to serve our country to the very limit of our ability.

Feeling as you did that your enlistment was the duty you owed your country and your flag, there was nothing else for you to do but to enlist. I want to be as ready to do my conscientious duty toward my country and my flag as you have shown yourself to be. And I rejoice that my country has allowed me to serve her in such a way that I do not have to disobey the dictates of my conscience in so doing. It makes my love for America and my devotion to her, always very real and very strong, all the stronger in these days of America's trial.

But oh! I am praying for the early coming of the day when such sacrifices as are being required today may no longer be necessary.

That God may hasten the coming of a just and permanent peace, and the reign of love and righteousness is my daily prayer.

May he keep you true to your highest ideals, save you from the dangers that you may have to meet, whether they be on the earth, in the air, or on the battlefield of your own spirit. And may you come back to us—I wish that it may be soon—strong and safe and clean in body and spirit, is the wish of your sincere friend,

(Levi T. Pennington)[12]

President Pennington's persistent drive to secure endowment, to increase enrollment, to develop a Quaker college that could adequately serve the church, to obtain a status of "Standard" for the college awakened an interest in him by other colleges. Because of this, the year 1917 may have provided his first genuine test of dedication to Pacific College. Early in the year he began to receive letters urging him to consider the possibility of succeeding President Edmund Stanley upon his expected retirement from Friends University in Wichita, Kansas. This idea was not totally new in January of 1917, because as early as September 28, 1915, William L. Pearson, principal of Friends University Biblical School, wrote to Pennington, ". . . you have been spoken of for the presidency of the most strategically located Friends College." During the first three months of the year he received a number of letters urging him to consider becoming a candidate for the presidency. On January 17 Gervas Carey, although still at Princeton, wrote urging Pennington to accept the presidency of Friends University if it were offered to him. On February 23 Lindley A. Wells, an evangelist and member of the board, wrote a confidential letter to President Pennington informing him that he could expect an offer of the presidency of Friends University, even suggesting a possible salary. The following day, February 24, W.S. Hadley, of the Citizens State Bank of Wichita, also a board member, wrote asking for permission to place Pennington's name before the College Board as a candidate for the presidency. The board meeting was scheduled for March 28, but consideration was being given to postponing it to accommodate the speaking schedule of Lindley Wells, who strongly wanted to be present at the meeting, presumably to speak in favor of the Pennington appointment. This was Hadley's second letter of inquiry in less than a month, and it appears from the letters that each man knew the other was also urging Levi T. Pennington to permit the use of his name as a candidate. On February 28 President Stanley also wrote to Pennington requesting permission to submit his name to the board as a candidate.

Edmund Stanley was believed to be seriously considering retirement. He had already devoted nearly fifty years to education, the last eighteen at Friends, and apparently the College Board fully expected him to announce his retirement in the spring, although this body was not requesting him to do so. However, he decided not to retire as expected, which resulted in a letter on March 14 from Hadley to Pennington informing him that Stanley was not now expected to retire as the board had expected.

The result was that a firm position did not materialize as it appeared, but the principle involving President Pennington was not altered by the temporary postponement of the position offer. However little or much private thought might have been given to opportunity elsewhere, no indication appears to remain that he seriously considered leaving Newberg. It is difficult to assess the merits of the respective positions, and particularly their special appeals to a man who was forced to weigh them against each other. But he responded in this situation as he was to respond to even more attractive opportunities later, that his call to Pacific College for service had not yet left him. And there is no indication of regretting his decision to remain despite the very seeming unsurmountable obstacles which Pacific College faced during the close of and immediately following the war, in 1918 and 1919.

The depth of Pennington's concern and the quality of his vision are distorted if a focus is narrowly kept upon his striving to simply keep the college in operation. He held to the conviction that a Quaker college holding to the principles of Friends could and must make a badly needed and unique contribution to the nation, to society, and to the church. He perceived that such a college could assist young people develop in such a way that their contribution would add a significant moral, spiritual, and intellectual ingredient to national life. And further, that if this quality of training were withheld from leadership, the nation would be weakened. It was this concern, this call to service that prompted him to sacrifice and ask for sacrifice of others to make such training possible for future leaders in all phases of society. One of his most stirring declarations and appeals was given in his report to the Yearly Meeting in 1918:

The present world situation calls for every man and woman to consider seriously and earnestly the personal question of personal duty. Great problems are facing the world today. Every man should make whatever contribution he can to their solution. But the greater problems still will confront the world when the present war is over and the race faces the problem of rebuilding a devastated world—a world laid waste industrially, financially, socially, morally, spiritually. The world, gone astray, must be led back to the right way, and the problem of leadership is the present and early future. The world must have a broad leadership, a capable leadership, a trained leadership, a Christian leadership.[13]

He believed this could be done for Quaker young people best by their attending a Quaker school, and he was most perplexed by the difficulty of securing the support from members of the Yearly Meeting in the most meaningful way: by influencing their youth to attend Pacific College. Continued low enrollments meant a constant need for supplementing tuition income for meeting the barest of operating costs. But the demands of the war and its effects reduced contributions. The reason for this is easy to understand, although for the college leadership it must have been regarded as ironical; perhaps the situation was too serious for irony, for it had within it the seeds of tragedy. The Friends, those who were expected to respond to the appeals for supporting one of their branches of service, their colleges, were also moved by the appeals for other grave world needs.

The Quakers were among the many agencies appealing for funds with which to feed the starving, displaced French and Belgians and those in other parts of the world. War had destroyed homes, so that shelter and clothing, medicine for fighting disease, all forms of humane relief were needed, and the Friends and their young people were participating in attempts to bring badly needed rehabilitation and relief to those abroad. It is understandable then that those who could give responded to these intense calls for help from the many agencies including the Friends who participated in war relief. President Pennington participated in relief programs so that he too understood the reason for negative responses to friends of the college who normally could be counted among those ready to give money to education.

Yet understanding, however admirable, could not satisfy the depleted college treasury for buying supplies, paying salaries, maintaining buildings, and improving the situation for the future.

It could not atone for the disappointment when a large number of individual invitations to give to the college were answered with the following typical response:

November 26, 1917

Levi T. Pennington
Pacific College, Oregon

Respected Friend

Thy appeal for funds to help support the work of Pacific College is at hand this morning and calls for a response.

The demands from all directions, particularly our own . . . and the toilers and sufferers in Europe as well as the starving in the far East, are so insistent that it is very difficult to administer to the necessities of all; and our great and growing West appears like a region from which help might be expected to *come* rather than to be drawing on our already over-taxed resources in the East.

I feel that I cannot well repeat the gift of two years ago, as so very much is expected here; but will enclose a small sum thus promptly, and hope a blessing will go with it.

Very truly thy friend,

(Elizabeth W. Garrett)[14]

The crucible years of Levi Pennington's administration were brought to a close with his eighth annual report to the Yearly Meeting in June 1919. This was the bleakest of his reports to date, if not of his thirty-year tenure. Almost every possible deterrent interfered with the 1918-1919 school year. The enrollment dropped to one of its lowest levels, for only in the first year of the college, 1891-1892 with 15 college students, 1893-1894 with 25, 1907-1908 with 22, had there been fewer than the 27 reported for 1918-1919. The wartime deficit posed a serious threat and was only countered with a special fund drive authorized by the board, which succeeded in raising something over $4,000 within the Oregon Yearly Meeting membership and just over $3,000 outside of its membership.

The war had depopulated the college of men students, partially because Pacific College did not have on campus a Students Army Training Corps, neither did it seek to obtain one. Another major reason for its depletion of students was explained in the annual report:

Some of our students went to schools that offered military training; Others went directly into the army and navy. While others have continued to go into our own denominational war relief service, under the American Friends Service Committee, in which work Pacific College is probably better represented, in proportion to the size of the student body, alumni and faculty, than any other college in the world.[15]

Still other problems had beset the school year just completed at the time of Pennington's report:

In addition to the difficulties which the war has presented, the influenza epidemic has presented its problems. The college opened two weeks late on account of the prune crop, which it seemed our duty to help in saving, for the sake of augmenting the world's food supply. After three weeks work we were closed by the authorities on account of the influenza peril, and for four weeks our work was interrupted. After resuming work, only a little over four weeks elapsed before we were again forced to close the college for some weeks. But in spite of all the difficulties and interruptions, we feel that a successful year's work has been done, for which we are truly grateful to God and to the friends of the college, who under his blessing, have made the work of the past year possible.[16]

To allow this to stand as a true picture of a small, struggling college is to engage in distortion. Only those who have participated in the life of a small, Christian college know of the close bond of fellowship that grows out of a bleak college situation. Some of the disadvantages within the educational contribution of a college in this condition can, in some measure, be compensated for by other kinds of development. This is not to advocate a meager educational experience as the ideal, yet it is an attempt to appreciate a quality of development that such a condition often produces. There is nothing more difficult than formulating a definition of education. No one would question the worth of an excellent, artistic plant with splendid equipment, learning resources, breadth of possible specialization, and a capable research faculty. However, the intangibles of education are so elusive that often they escape the tight net thrown around the students by a campus that has only the material evidences of an educational process. The process itself, the growth in perspective, the maturity of judgment, the fulfillment of the creative impulse, all of which resides as the dynamic of the educational process, cannot easily be put into motion. All too frequently this dynamic has been expressed through the lives of graduates who have been trained in what appears to have been too limited an environment. There is every reason to believe that President Pennington nurtured a faith in this perspective of education, and that even those cruel years of crucible experiences could not dissuade him from his commitments to the education of young Friends whose service to the world was badly needed.

Notes to Chapter II

1. The Reagan letters are from the Family Papers (FP).
2. *OYM Minutes*, 1912, p. 25
3. (FP).
4. (FP).
5. (FP).
6. *OYM Minutes*, 1912, p. 28.
7. Letters to Rebecca are from the Family Papers.
8. *OYM Minutes*, 1913, pp. 24-25.
9. *OYM Minutes*, 1914, p. 23.
10. *OYM Minutes*, 1916, p. 19.
11. *OYM Minutes*, 1917, p. 16.
12. (FP).
13. *OYM Minutes*, 1918, pp. 34-35.
14. (FP).
15. *OYM Minutes*, 1919, p. 25.
16. *OYM Minutes*, 1919, p. 25.

CHAPTER

III

Minister
at
Large

1919-1931

IN THE TWELVE-YEAR PERIOD between the summer of 1919
and 1931, Levi Pennington participated in an ever-widening range
of service. During the first two years of this period he was released from the presidency of Pacific College to direct a movement
within the Society of Friends which attempted to unite several
groups within the Quaker movement in America in promoting
church growth, assist church efforts in foreign and American missions, and raise money to promote Quaker education. Upon his
return to the college in 1921 he was in great demand as a speaker
throughout the United States, and is said to have become the most
popular speaker in the state of Oregon. He was released from the
college again for the 1930-31 school year to serve Quaker interests
in the United States, England, and Ireland. Because of this new extension to his reputation and influence, especially in this period of
his life, it seems best characterized as a decade and more of serving
as a "Minister at Large." This designation is used both in its narrower and broader sense, because his preaching was nationwide,
and his speaking and writing were also widely recognized. He was
in great demand as a preacher, as a commencement speaker, by
service groups, and by professional groups such as lawyers, newspaper editors, and educators. His topics ranged from Mother's
Day sermons, discussions of the peace issue, championing the
cause of temperance, the purposes of education, problems in
athletics, to moral issues in the practice of law, and the responsibilities of newspaper editors.

Two years as director of the Forward Movement resulted in his becoming well-known among the bodies of the Quaker movement, and curiously appears to have contributed to a general widening of his reputation beyond the church itself. This enhancing of his reputation provided opportunities through which his contribution as a vigorous voice for moral responsibility in society elevated his life to a high level of significance, both to the Friends Church and to the state of Oregon. In a restricted sense Jesus' words, "A prophet is not without honor save in his own country," are applicable to Pennington, for perhaps his bitterest verbal battles with resulting alienations from co-workers occurred at home. Yet despite these bitter encounters and the memory of them in impressionable minds and emotions, he was honored in his home community. Frequently his intensity, his harshness, and his cutting responses, both polarized a meeting in its attitudes toward him and elicited a paradoxical esteem and fear of him among his students and friends.

It is unfortunate that discussions of movements within church groups cannot be made clear without historical background, but a brief story of Levi Pennington's life cannot include a history of Quakerism and its very complex history in America. The Friends movement began in the middle decades of the 17th century in England under the preaching of George Fox. It has undergone many changes in its three centuries of life, but its high regard for individualism and complete autonomy, resulting from an insistence upon something of God within all men, has tended to fragment the movement. For one wishing an orientation to Quakerism in order to see Pennington's assignment in clearer perspective, the *Handbook of the Religious Society of Friends* is a helpful resource as well as the *Friends Directory*. The continuous change within the Society of Friends quickly makes any history of contemporary Friends outdated, but *American Quakers Today*, edited by Edwin B. Bronner of Haverford College (1965), although being superseded, provides an invaluable background for this chapter in Pennington's life.

In the summer of 1919, the Five Years Meeting of Friends appointed President Pennington to direct a movement which sought to develop unified drives and promote areas of vital concern to Friends within their persuasion. The Five Years Meeting, so called, was organized in 1902 at Richmond, Indiana, by twelve yearly meetings who had previously adopted the Richmond Declaration of Faith, issued in 1887 by Friends who sought greater unity in purpose and practise: New England, New York, Baltimore, Canada, Wilmington (in Ohio), Indiana, Western (in Indiana), Iowa, Kansas, California, Oregon, and North Carolina. The geographical configuration has been subject to a great deal of change because of some yearly meetings withdrawing and others affiliating with it, but preservation of this basic organization resulted in a name change in 1965 to Friends United Meeting. However, the Five Years Meeting as now the Friends United Meeting cooperated with other groups of Friends so that Levi Pennington as director of the Forward Movement became known to nearly the entire Quaker movement in the United States and Canada.

A statement of the purposes of this movement as they were reported in the *Handbook of the Five Years Meeting in America* (1921) is necessary in any evaluation of Pennington's accomplishments during this period of his directorship. These purposes as reported in the *Handbook* are given in the following paragraph:

The Friends Forward Movement must be understood as an auxiliary agent for the assistance of the established organs of the church rather than an organization of itself. It is interested in evangelism, in which the Board of Home Missions is interested, because it is an essential and fundamental mission of the church. It is interested in lifework recruits, because these are an interest of the Five Years Meeting. It is interested in intercession and stewardship of property, not because of any peculiar relation to these interests, but because these too are a common interest of the whole church and of all the boards. It is not interested in raising money for itself, except in so far as it is necessary to carry on the work of coordination of interests. It is not supplanting in any way the Boards and established organs of the society, but is merely carrying on this coordination of their interests. Its purpose is nothing more nor less than to serve the Society by re-emphasizing the message of direct personal relationship with God and direct personal service to humanity, of enlisting the membership of Friends in a great fellowship of intercession for God's blessing upon his work and especially upon that portion of his work entrusted to the Friends, the helping of all to meet open-eyed and honestly the responsibilities in this day, the interpreting in terms of men and money Friends in carrying on the work of God through evangelism laying a special emphasis upon the enlistment of life-work recruits, and lastly the raising by united campaign a budget adequate to the united task of Friends.[1]

The initial discussions which led within a few months to the development of the Forward Movement began with a four-day conference in the home of David M. Edwards early in January 1919, with representatives from coast to coast. These approximately twenty-five representatives laid the foundation upon which the Executive Committee of the Five Years Meeting established the movement by selecting Levi Pennington, one of its own members, as its director.

The announcement of his appointment issued to the church reads:

To Friends to whom this may concern:-

Levi T. Pennington, a member of Oregon Yearly Meeting, and a minister of the Gospel held in high esteem, has been selected as Director of the Forward Movement among Friends in America, by the Five Years Meeting which has been charged with the responsibility of maturing plans for this very important enterprise.

Of the two general divisions into which the work falls, namely, (1) the proclaiming of the message of the gospel as understood by Friends, and (2) the organization of our members to meet the new opportunities now opening before us, it is felt that the first-named task is in reality first in importance, and we doubt not that the Director of the work will feel the need of the largest possible measure of assistance on the part of Friends to whom he may come in preparing the way both for the Gospel service as the Holy Spirit may lead, and for the presentation to meetings and to individuals of the plans for the work as they may be matured.

As a servant of the Lord dedicated by the church to take a place of leadership in this time of unusual opportunity for organized, co-operative service in carrying the message of Christ to the world, we commend Levi T. Pennington to your Christian care, and are in love with your friends.

Signed on behalf of the Committee in charge of the Forward Movement among Friends in America,

Allen D. Hole

Chairman of the Executive Committee
of the Five Years Meeting of the Friends in America[2]

Judging from the reports which he submitted to official bodies and the wholehearted enthusiasm with which he entered into these new responsibilities, it can be concluded that Pennington entered into his directorship with a feeling of excitement and challenge. It was an opportunity to work toward strengthening the particular areas of the church in which he was vitally interested. Although he was on leave, correspondence indicates that he was uncertain whether he would return to the college as he had planned.

He was undoubtedly gratified by letters from the college constituency which expressed both regret that he was leaving the college and fear that he might not return. One such letter reads in part:

Homedale, Idaho
August 31st, 1919

Dear Penningtons,

I've taken a long time to consider whether I was really glad you were leaving Oregon Yr. Mtg. for even a little while but after thinking it all over, reading what you and the Am. Friend had to say 'I am glad' to each of your glad questions.

I do not like to think of P.C. or Oregon Yr. Mtg. without any of you but have confidence in your ability to decide what is right and I think I truly desire the best possible for Am. Quakerism. . . . I do wish your family, each and all success in your undertakings at this time. I could wish I felt confident of your return in a year—only time can tell.

. . . I do hope they find the right man for 'Acting Pres.'

Glad to have known you all and we shall be interested, vitally, in what you do and tho among the least we are with the 'Forward Movement.'

Truly your friend,

Anna W. Benson[3]

Levi Pennington received substantial support from members of the faculty who felt a strong bond of fellowship with him in the work of the college, and who could not look to the immediate future of the college optimistically with the haunting fear that he might not return to Newberg. This fear was expressed especially by those who were at this time furthering their education by attending graduate school, and especially when receiving teaching opportunities elsewhere. Russell W. Lewis, a professor of English, was attending graduate school at the University of California. He was a very close friend of Levi; both were avid fishermen who fished Oregon streams together. They shared the common bond of excitement as lovers of literature, and they both possessed imaginative minds which found stimulation in subtle forms of keen intellectual wit. This strong bond cemented their friendship despite rather differing personalities, and their correspondence reflects this warm understanding. Perhaps of all the thousands of letters to friends written during his lifetime, none reflect quite the same relaxed, self-revealing attitudes as those to Professor Lewis. Each man wrote to the other with all defensive guards down, unafraid of revealing his weaknesses and stating his insecurities. It is out of this context that letters between these men must be understood, for their significance lies within the candid nature of their expressed judgment and reaction to situation. In a long, handwritten letter to Pennington from Berkeley on January 13, 1920, Russell Lewis wrote:

> My! What a job we have undertaken in the Forward Movement! And what a blessing it will be to the church, and the world! I just got the Jan. 8th American Friend today, and I have some very interesting reading ahead of me in that account of the Forward Movement.

> I am, as it were, holding my breath until I can hear whether or not you will be back to P.C. next year. I don't suppose you know yet, so I am not *asking. I am just expressing an unusual amount of interest in the question. Of course I want you back, yet that may not be the biggest piece of service you can give, and if it is not, I suppose you should not be there. I confess I do not much relish the prospect of teaching at P.C. without the very pleasant associations with the Penningtons which we have so much leaned upon.*[4]

One cannot use letters from close friends to argue for a lament of the faculty over Pennington's appointment which took him to Richmond, Indiana, but the faculty members upon whom the burden of carrying on the work of the college fell, those who were better preparing themselves for effective service appear to have expressed the same sentiments as Lewis.

This relationship between Russell Lewis and Levi Pennington reveals a quality of LTP's life which is sometimes hidden, namely, that he was a trusted counselor. His advice was frequently sought by those who were quite apart from life at Newberg and Pacific College. Speakers who had appeared in Oregon wrote for an honest evaluation of their efforts, others consulted him concerning personal decisions. For this reason the following exchange between these men is representative. Frequently other such exchanges concern problems that should not be given public exposure:

Mist, California
May 14, 1920

Dear Pennington:

Is it as disagreeable for you as for me to dwell in the Valley of Indecision? That has been our address since we received a letter from Pres. McGrew a few days ago asking if I would consider a proposition of coming to Penn [William Penn College in Iowa] to replace Professor Harris in the English Department. I have been wishing all day that I had written you immediately to ask for your good advice. Pres. McGrew did not say what work I would be expected to handle, and I have written to ask him if my teaching would be entirely in the college department, and about the salary. He thought the salary might be made $1800. I did not commit myself to him, though, because of my contract with Pacific College. If Pres. Mills is willing to release me, we are very much in the notion of going— without yet being *sure* that it is the best thing to do. Consulting only our *emotions*, there is little reason for moving. It does seem the *reasonable* thing to do, though, if I am to teach a few more years longer. It seems that this is a good chance to begin going forward; for I am beginning to see the advantages of getting somewhere in the profession, both from the standpoint of business success, and of capacity to serve. Pacific College has done much for me, but she cannot fully *make* me a teacher. So I really feel that to go to Penn would be a wise move. On the other hand we do not like to think of leaving Oregon where our friends, and especially our parents, live. Oregon looks good to us as a 'homeland.' And the fishing is bully in *Oregon!* So it is a difficult quandry to get out of. Pres. McGrew may get us out though, by writing that *they* want me to work in the Penn Academy, which I am not willing to do; or Pres. Mills may say no to the proposition and keep me at P.C. next year. Do you know definitely, or nearly so, what we ought to do? If you do, I wish you would tell us, and save us the pain of deciding, for, really the Valley of Indecision is no pleasant place for me.

If rest and leisure were transferable, I would be willing to divide with you, for I imagine you are still leaning into the collar on that up-hill pull. I have been out here nearly two weeks now, loafing considerably, and working only barely enough to allow me to approach the 'family board' with some semblance of a clear conscience. I couldn't exaggerate the feeling of relief with which I finish the Semester's work and come to my family. But I don't need to describe it to you. I found them all well here, and the children seem to be taking advantage of the good climate, for they are growing and developing remarkably fast. Even Constance has lost nearly every evidence of babyhood—except the dialect. I wish you could hear her sing, 'Away down 'touse in Dickey.' (But the fond *payrent* must abandon this see-dencing subject.) Eula is still teaching, and cannot finish the term before July 9. That is a source of some regret, for I shall have to go back to B. alone, and wait for three weeks for the rest of us to come. That will give us only three weeks together in town.

I am in a fair way now to finish up my work by Aug. 1. I have yet to make one hour of credit, pass the Eng. Finals in Hist. of the Lang., Theories of Prose and Poetry, and a Special Author (my Thesis man, Blake), and finish my thesis. I am working some now on the history of the language, and hope to get quite a bit of thesis work done before going back to school June 21. I don't know yet how well I made in my examinations. I think I 'got by' (for that is a much-used phrase at U. of C. among the 'great unwashed,' and I came near qualifying for admission into that despised order in the Middle English Course!)

I was fortunate enough to pull a 1 out of the Eng. Finals in Oral and Written Expression. My undergraduate courses were all easy excepting the Mid. Eng., which was for me a good deal of a plunge 'into the depths.' The year's work has been a much greater experience than I had hoped. Even if I should never teach again I should not regret it, and I have learned a good deal about Eng. Lit. and English departments. . . .

Sincerely yours, Russell W. Lewis

Pennington's response follows:

May 23, 1920

Prof. R.W. Lewis   Mist, California

Dear Friend:

I do not just know the location of your home there but it certainly seems that it must be in the Valley of Indecision unless it has been rechristened and by this time is the Valley of Decision. No, I do not either know definitely or nearly so what you ought to do. It looks like a fine offer from Penn. If Pacific can take care of the job there it would seem from your own standpoint that you ought to go. I can't think of it with any kind of comfort but my own future is so unsettled that it might be possible you would be nearer me in the future years at Oskaloosa than at Newberg.

I would be entirely willing to share your rest and leisure with you if it were possible to divide up. There seems no immediate prospect of any real layoff for me. If I am well enough to give a Commencement address at Spiceland Academy day after tomorrow, speak at Westfield Quarterly Meeting Saturday, give the Memorial Day address in the Old Brick Church at Wabash Sunday and that night leave Chicago for Central City, Nebraska on my way to Pacific Commencement and Oregon Yearly Meeting.

I am glad prospects are so good for completing the work for your Master's Degree by the 1st of August.

I am getting no time whatever these days to work on my two remaining courses for my Oregon University Master's Degree. I have my work done in Contemporary English Novelist, about half done with one or two hours more to make in Original Verse, then my thesis and then, well that's still a long way off.

It has been definitely decided to continue the Forward Movement but the new Committee is only partly formed and there has been no decision as to who will be the director next year. It was certainly an interesting time when the report was made and there are difficulties ahead for the next year perhaps no greater but certainly almost as great and perplexing as those of the first year. What my relationship with the Movement will be remains as yet undetermined. I should judge however that there would be no chance of my being back in Oregon the coming year.

With kindest regards and with very best wishes from all the Penningtons to all the Lewises, I am

Sincerely your friend,

(LTP)[6]

The role of a Minister at Large pressed him into a wearing speaking schedule even more demanding than his allusion in Lewis's letter indicates. For example, he spoke at the Penn College commencement at 10:00 Tuesday morning, June 1, on "Lightening," then umpired a baseball game in the afternoon in which the Penn Alumni won over the college seven to five, followed in the evening with an address, "Be Thou an Example," to the Meeting of Ministry and Oversight of Iowa Yearly Meeting. The following morning he spoke to the Yearly Meeting on "Jesus of Nazareth, King of the Jews." On Friday he gave the educational address in the forenoon, and was scheduled to give the annual class sermon to the graduating class of the Astoria (Oregon) High School Commencement June 6. Following this appearance he was due to retrace his steps back to the midwest for an address on evangelism to Western Yearly Meeting in Indiana June 28. Judging from other time periods for which complete daily schedules are available, any conservative reconstruction of his time not spent on the train would suggest that he also met additional speaking engagements while in Oregon.

Although Pennington loved to speak, he also liked to write. All who knew him were aware of this continuous preoccupation, although probably only a few of his closer associates knew of his ambitions to write mystery stories, drama, and fiction. He was highly motivated to write articles for periodicals, and it is this high degree of motivation that makes his exchange of letters with Marcia Doan, editor of *The Quaker*, such a significant commentary upon the strenuous schedule which Levi was keeping during these days of promoting the activities of the Forward Movement in 1920. An exchange of three letters in August and September of this year in themselves provide an unusual commentary upon his schedule and consequent reordering of his usual priorities:

Philadelphia
Eighth Month, 20. 1920

Levi Pennington,
Pacific College,
Newberg, Oregon

Dear Friend:

Thee is doubtless somewhat familiar with our new journal THE QUAKER, copies of which have already been sent thee.

It is our purpose in this publication to furnish a medium for a stimulating interchange of thought upon the broad fundamental principles which form the rich heritage of all Friends, regardless of any particular branch. In order to cling steadfastly to this high plane, we must have represented the best in Quakerism,—the broadest, keenest thought interpreted in articles written by the present day leaders of our society. For this reason we are extremely anxious that thee be represented in one of our early issues. We are looking to thee for a leading article on some subject which thee deems appropriate. The articles already written by Hoover, Sproul and Palmer, may give thee an idea as to the general type and length, about two-thousand words.

May we not receive a favorable reply from thee in the near future?

Sincerely thine,

Marcia Doan[7]

Pennington's reply seems surprising, particularly in the light of this opportunity to join the other prominent men named as recent contributors:

Aug. 30, 1920

Marcia Doan
The Quaker
152 W. 15th St.
Philadelphia, Pa.

Dear Friend:

Your letter of Eighth Month 20th directed to me at Pacific College, Newberg, Oregon, has just reached me.

While I appreciate the invitation you have given me to write an article for The Quaker in the near future I doubt very much my ability to make such a thing possible in view of the tasks that are already upon me in connection with the Forward Movement. I have found it almost impossible to write the material that was absolutely required for our Forward Movement News and the other things which seemed vital I should write for the American Friend. It does not seem to me that it would be wise for you to depend upon an article from me at any time in the near future.

Again assuring you of my appreciation of the invitation, I am

Sincerely your friend,

(Levi T. Pennington)[8]

Marcia Doan appeared undaunted in her early reply to Pennington's letter, for she responded with a logic and firmness that characterizes the strong, historical Quaker woman of action transformed almost into flesh and blood before a reader's eye by the pictorial portrait of the Quaker figure associated with her use of the familiar language.

Philadelphia   Ninth Month, 16th, 1920

Levi T. Pennington,
220 Colonial Bldg.,
Richmond, Ind.

Dear Friend:

Thank thee so much for thy letter of 8 Mo. 30th. I can readily appreciate that, in view of the important work that thee is doing, thy time is at a premium. However, the fact that thee is engaged in this work means that thee would have much to say of a great benefit to our readers. We hope, therefore, to receive an article some time in the future, and are earnestly wishing that we will not have to wait long.

Very sincerely thine,

Marcia Doan
Editor[9]

An attempt to give an appraisal of Levi Pennington's contribution to the Society of Friends as a result of his two years as director of the Forward Movement is filled with peril, and ought not to be undertaken if any definitive statement were to be issued. It is safest to give a statement of his activities and leave any generalization to a reader, although some indication of his accomplishments and those of his co-workers in the Movement are necessary in a responsible estimation of his life. There are some sources of information which should provide at least a fairly dependable evaluation of his work. Apart from the Pennington Papers in the University of Oregon Collection, there are approximately 2,000 pages of reports by the Movement, letters to and from the director concerning its strengths and weaknesses, and related information concerning its cooperation with other organs of the Society. There is also the 1921 report of Walter C. Woodward, general secretary of the Five Years Meeting, in which he summarized the accomplishments of the Forward Movement. Further, interviews with at least a few who were in leadership positions in the 1920 era, and with others who were leaders sometime afterward, both in the Five Years Meeting and among other Quaker groups, convey a positive attitude toward its successes. These appraisals were matters of judgment, and a definition of success in this kind of endeavor is frequently a matter of perspective. Some look back upon the Movement and express weak praise for it, others can cite developments and gains which are still evident. These appraisals find no fault with the objectives; some wonder how many of them were reached, and if the alienations which developed as negative reactions to its methods outweighed its benefits.

These differing views notwithstanding, Woodward's published summary of the Movement's activities is quite impressive. Anyone who works for the church or other agency involving what might be called acts of faith must believe that the many publications, personal contacts, conferences with college and secondary young people, raising operating funds, and evangelistic campaigns carried on under the supervision of the Movement must have resulted in good. There can be little doubt that more people were reached in an influential way than would have been had the Forward Movement not existed. Its thrust and influence is to Pennington's credit.

In the report of the Executive Committee of the Five Years Meeting (April 1921), a summary of the college visitations and individual conferences held by the Life Work Deputation group within the Forward Movement shows:[10]

College	Number of Interviews
Earlham	28
Friends University	21
Nebraska Central	24
Penn	48
Wilmington	18
Guilford	40

Visits were also made to Oakwood School, Westtown School, and Oberlin College. These visitations were made by Clarence E. Pickett with the exception of Guilford College, where he was assisted by Samuel E. Haworth, Kirby V. Bowen, and Ross A. Hadley. Faculty members from each college gave assistance because these were usually two- and three-day conferences in which students were challenged to consider a life work in a number of callings associated with human service: teaching, the ministry, religious work, medical, prison work, boys' work, law, as well as service through business, engineering, and agriculture.

These conferences were undertaken for fulfilling the goal of the Movement of enlisting life-work recruits, but there is no way of measuring the outcome of these personal conferences, nor of determining how many college students responded to the public challenges issued during these college visitations usually opening with a chapel address followed by smaller group meetings held by student organizations. More general accomplishments were summarized by Walter Woodward in his report after "One Year of Co-operative Effort."

> As evidence of these results we point to the achievements of the first year of the kind of co-operative effort of which we have been speaking. The Forward Movement was launched and carried on primarily as a great spiritual enterprise. As such it brought an awakening in the prayer life of the membership, to the claims of evangelism, to our responsibility as Christian stewards both of life and of property. The proof of this awakening was found in the financial ingathering. Religious experience and large giving for religious work may not always be mutually expressive, each of the other. But when a membership in whole or in large part rises to new heights of sacrificial giving, it is evidence that an experience worthwhile has come to it. It is from this point of view that we are presenting this general statement as a preface to the report of the boards. In speaking of the financial phases and accomplishments of the year, we are not ignoring the great objectives of the church toward which they aim. We are dealing here with the means whereby objectives may be attained; with the measure of our Christian devotion.

> In response to the first united and simultaneous financial appeal made in the spring of 1920 under the auspices of the Forward Movement, more money was contributed for the support of our common work than the church had ever known. Not only this, but each and every department of work received more funds during the year than in any previous year. The aggregate giving for the year reached a total of approximately $375,000. For the first time in the history of some of our boards, instead of having to spend nervous energy and effort in raising funds, they were free to give attention to the actual work which we expect of them.[11]

One might say that Walter C. Woodward strongly favored organizing the Forward Movement, and that consequently his appraisal of its accomplishments may lack objectivity. However, these two paragraphs are only secondarily reporting on the Movement. For the most part this is only a statement to remind members of the Five Years Meeting that cooperation is the key for accomplishing the goals of the church. As such it is a reminder of what was already known.

A more telling statement concerning the Forward Movement is contained in the opening paragraph of another section of the same report entitled "What of the Future?" This is a much more biting statement used to point out weaknesses inherent in the unsystematic approaches to meeting church goals. Here the accomplishments of the Forward Movement are reviewed to dramatize the plight of the Five Years Meeting now that it lacked some form of cooperative effort as was carried on systematically under Pennington's direction.

> Despite the objectionable features of the Forward Movement financial campaign, as a matter of fact it actually worked in a very large measure, as we have already shown. Through a simultaneous, centrally directed effort, the church was awakened spiritually and financially; the money raised for Christian enterprises far exceeded anything in our history. This year we have stepped out by faith in the more Quakerly way. The United Budget Campaign, while promoted from the central office, is actually in the hands of the Yearly Meetings. With them is the initiative. With them lies the success or failure of our common work. In place of a simultaneous campaign in its own way and in its own time. There is lacking, therefore, the momentum, the contagious enthusiasm which comes with a simultaneous united effort. Long before this time last year, the financial campaign was practically accomplished and a large part of the subscriptions paid, for carrying the work steadily forward. This year, in but few Yearly Meetings has the campaign been pushed to a conclusion. Our fiscal year is one third gone, yet the funds so far received are so inconsequential as to be almost negligible. The whole program of the church is most seriously threatened. As evidence of this, the Foreign Mission Board is not able to return to the field its missionaries now home on furlough and has sent out instructions for radical retrenchment on the field.[12]

Upon returning to Pacific College for the 1921-22 academic year President Pennington once more resumed efforts toward gaining accreditation for the college. A successful drive to raise money for paying off indebtedness had placed the college in a situation for buying additional equipment prerequisite for gaining recognition by the Bureau of Education. Consequently, early in the school year college authorities sought to obtain an inspection by the United States Bureau of Education. However, it was not until March 16 that the inspector actually arrived, but the report based upon the inspection did not reach the college until May 23. This meant that after complying with various requirements issued by the Bureau, the college administration waited for an entire school year before learning if the rating of "Standard" were any nearer than before. The visitation resulted in a clearer statement of Bureau requirements than had been spelled out in previous years, but in his report to the Yearly Meeting the president made a statement of hope, but with no prediction. It was not until three and one-half years later that Levi was able to send the following wire to Rebecca:

> December 12, 1925
>
> Mrs. L.T. Pennington
> 1000 Sheridan Street
> Newberg, Oregon
>
> United States Bureau of Education recognizes Pacific as Standard College.
>
> Levi T. Pennington[13]

In returning to Pacific College in 1921, the returning president did not step back into the same stream from which he had waded two years earlier. He returned to many of the same problems, took up once again many of the same pressures of administration and teaching, but he began a new era of statewide recognition. His services as a speaker were in constant demand, yet these public appearances added to his load. His schedule now testifies to his great strength and capacity for heavy work loads.

In his first letter back to his friends in Richmond, Indiana, Mr. and Mrs. Willis Beebe, Pennington gave an account of his life after returning to the college (October 20, 1921). This is representative of his many letters to friends during the decade of the 1920s; it shows excitement in his return to the college, and a continuing stimulation from his speaking schedule:

> There has been an increase of about 25% over the attendance of a year ago and that has made more work for everybody. There has been some new equipment to buy in various departments and I am teaching two hours more per week than I had first thought would

be possible. I have some of the finest classes I have ever had. Seven in philosophy, 14 in Shakespeare, 17 in public speaking, and 11 in college Bible. All of these are three hour classes except public speaking, a two hour class.

In addition to all the work here at the college, I have found plenty to do outside. Yesterday was two addresses before the students in a public school. The 14th it was an address on education (and incidentally on peace and disarmament) before the Grange Fair at Scholls. October 12 it was an address on peace and disarmament before the State WCTU Convention (and after the address they passed unanimously a resolution that every union is to circulate petitions in favor of disarmament). October 9 it was a sermon at Springbrook. October 2 it was two sermons at Portland. September 28 it was an address to the Young Mens Christian Association. September 21 it was the opening chapel. Other chapels don't count but I have plenty of them.

And on ahead are three addresses before the County Teachers Institute at McMinnville on the 27th, an address before the County Christian Endeavor Convention on the 29th, an address on peace and disarmament in the Portland Public Library, date not yet fixed, a probable address . . . at Seattle November 4 and 5, and other things in prospect of less consequence perhaps, but all of them taking time and energy.[14]

Despite such a schedule, Pennington took time for sharing the concerns of a sensitive, understanding man of faith. In a moment of need by friends he wrote an unusually tender and understanding letter of sympathy and understanding:

May 1, 1922

Rev. and Mrs. Robert E. Pretlow
2315 E. Spruce Street
Seattle, Washington

Dear Friends:

I have just read the letter which you wrote to the Sutton family telling of the home going of little Bobby. I do not know what it is like to face such a loss. I think nobody can know who has not passed through the actual experience. But as I think of it and realize that time and imagination are very little of what the actuality must be, my heart goes out to you all in sympathy. May the God to whom I believe that little Bobby has gone, be with you and comfort and sustain you all. If you can convey my sincere sympathy to the boy's parents without hurting more than it helps, I wish you would do so.

When I face such things as these with the inevitable 'why', I simply have to try to draw near to God and trust where I cannot understand. Not only from the standpoint of faith but from the standpoint of actual utility, though that seems a poor word for such a case. The words contained in your letter is the best philosophy I know, 'The Lord gave and the Lord hath taken away, Blessed be the name of the Lord.'

I trust that your heart, Mrs. Pretlow, may not be left too much desolate. We do not know what it is on the other side, but certain I am that God does not let the kind of value represented by little Bobby be lost for ever. He is not lost even to you. He is taken from you for awhile—the world of spiritual things is surely more real than the world of microbes and death.

May God sustain you all. I would not worry you with many words but you all have my sympathy and my prayers and my heart aches with yours, the father and mother, and all the grandparents.

Rebecca and the girls join in sincere sympathy as do all your Newberg friends I am sure.

Sincerely your friend,

(Levi T. Pennington)[15]

During this period of Levi Pennington's life, Pacific College experienced some optimistic developments that should be placed in perspective with the continued financial strain often associated with this era. Gaining the long-sought recognition of "Standard" by the Bureau of Education provided a new basis for a brighter future; however, as Ralph Beebe aptly pointed out in his summary of this decade in A Garden of the Lord, many major obstacles continued to threaten its existence. The long drama which had been playing out the history of the college since before Pennington's arrival in 1911 continued to maintain its suspense by holding the question of mere survival up to its public. There seemed no way to introduce a new motif, the theme of margin. The ideals of a more sustaining enrollment, an improved library and instructional equipment, a better trained faculty, and a measure of financial security seemed always to elude the administration and faculty. Standardization certainly climaxed an all-important chapter in this history. But a look backward shows another significant development taking place: a consistent upward trend in enrollment. The enrollment moved upward year by year with only an occasional drop, as opposed to the pre-1920s. In 1921-22 the enrollment in the college was 47 and continued to rise. Only in 1927-28 and 1928-29 did losses occur, but in 1929-30 enrollments began again higher than the 1928 level. By 1934 the college registered 92 students.

Ironically, this was to be another plateau, not a sustained trend to the 500 student dream of the earlier decade. These decades of minimum operation raise haunting questions in the mind of anyone examining Pennington's life and administration. Why did he remain with the college? Why was it so difficult to establish the college on a more effective level? Were those who were within its management too close to observe it in comparison with like colleges, and thereby too quickly satisfied? Or was the constituency actually too small to provide for a college operation? The history of the college itself suggests some answers. One is that reports all indicate that Oregon Yearly Meeting believed so strongly in carrying on a Christian college that the idea of maintaining even a small, struggling college was more comforting than the thought of not providing young Friends with training in the Society's principles. Another belief seems to have sustained these efforts; namely, that a future yet awaited the college, if the Board of Managers and all participating groups could hold on to this thread of faith. The simple, direct answer to this question as it relates to Pennington is summarized by his frequent statement during the later years of his life that God had called him to Pacific College and had not yet released him from that call.

These responses seem all too idealized to stand before contemporary systems of analysis which subject all operations to standards of efficiency and accountability. But from these painful years of beginning and struggle, years of foundation laying, Pacific College (christened later George Fox College) emerged as a college in which the Yearly Meeting could feel even Quakerly pride. Again it is from history that both an answer and a vindication emerges to the haunting and enigmatic questions easily raised of this early epoch, and of Pennington's continued attempts to build a recognized college of liberal studies.

President Pennington completed his master's degree in English at the University of Oregon in the spring of 1922, a commendable feat considering his heavy load of administration, teaching, and speaking. He always considered this as one of his most satisfying accomplishments, and when his course papers are read in comparison with contemporary "critical" graduate papers his satisfaction appears well justified. It was not unusual for him to take issue with an instructor's critique by writing a lengthy essay in rebuttal to criticism. These dialogues comprise a window for viewing LTP's personality in a light that only a few friends appeared to appreciate. He loved to spar, verbally, with anyone who held a judgment differing from his. His aggressive, competitive spirit would not let him be the loser until he was persuaded that he was in error, which occasionally occurred; however, this resolution of differences seldom took place in public. Now, many of those who observed him in these public disputations realize that he was a victim of his own zeal, that he was too protective of his own ego. It now becomes clear that despite the weaknesses which this tendency produced in him, it was also the brick and mortar of his critical judgments which gave him a standing with the state university, and kept him fighting for the survival of an almost hopeless educational cause. Viewed from this perspective, Pennington stands forth as any leader dedicated to a high calling, he was man—paradoxical, quixotic, eyes raised heavenward, but with feet of clay.

The "Minister at Large" era closed with his release from the college for the 1930-31 school year to minister among Eastern Quakers with three months spent with Rebecca in England and Ireland. This was a year full of engagements among yearly meetings in the Midwest and along the Atlantic. He gave nearly 250 sermons and addresses and participated in many additional services. Frequently Rebecca also spoke in meetings of worship as they visited monthly meetings. In reporting on his activities during this term of released service he noted:

> We were in eighteen meetings in Western Yearly Meeting, nine in Indiana Yearly Meeting, and sixteen in New York Yearly Meeting.

> We spent the time from November 1 to December 21 among Friends in Philadelphia and Baltimore Yearly Meetings. Nearly all our service in Pennsylvania and New Jersey being among Arch Street Friends. We were in forty-nine sittings in Philadelphia Yearly Meeting and its subordinate meetings and sixteen in Baltimore Yearly Meeting and its subordinate meetings.

We spent the month of February in the limits of New England Yearly Meeting; however, we were in forty-five sittings and last of these among the Conservative Friends of Western Rhode Island with whom we had very happy service.

In England we were in ninety gatherings, in parlor meetings, meetings for worship, yearly, quarterly, and monthly meetings, and in mass meetings in numerous places.

In Ireland we had similar experiences where we were in thirty-three gatherings, yearly meetings, parlor meetings, mass meetings, meetings for worship, school meetings, and others, including one street meeting.[16]

During this twelve-year period President Pennington served as a true minister at large through his influence in advancing moral values into the community beyond the church. His stature as a speaker provided him with opportunities for addressing many different groups and professions, and he used his appearances for advocating the same moral perspectives that characterized his speaking in the churches.

Two such addresses are used in concluding this chapter for a reader to observe firsthand something of his hard-hitting methods. The first was given to the Association of Independent Colleges of Oregon, an organization in which he was active over many years, having served as its president more than once. Most of the colleges in this organization were religious in orientation, although not all. But the latter could be expected to appreciate the values which Pennington advocated in his address; consequently, his emphasis upon the importance of religion would have been both expected and appreciatively received. In a sense he was on his own ground.

In contrast, his true character is better revealed through the second address, for in it a reader can see that he did not tone down his message for groups which might be antagonistic to his moral stance. In this address before the Oregon Bar Association he demonstrates his courage by his uncompromising attitude. In it he urged members of the Bar to develop stronger moral consciousness through integrity and lives which sought to influence young people in their respect for law. When speaking for other groups Pennington was equally forthright.

THE PLACE OF RELIGION IN OUR
EDUCATIONAL PROGRAM

(For the program of the Association of Independent Colleges of Oregon, 1925.)

As I was about to say, with so vast a subject and one of such tremendous importance I shall be like the man who was given five minutes to talk on the Mississippi Valley, and who remarked that he did not expect fully to cover his subject.

Permit three preliminary remarks.

First, religion is normal. We do not all mean the same thing when we say, "Man is incurably religious." But though some seem to have discovered the chaulmoogra oil to cure the incurable, yet it is true that every normal man, woman and child has certain religious instincts which are as normal as those supposedly basic ones of feeding, fearing and fighting.

We do not all have the same theories, but theories are after all not the most important things in the world. Ether or no ether, radio works. A man might have no knowledge of the kinetic theory of gases, and might even deny that theory, but might still be able to run an automobile. Some of us may hold that by religion man climbs back to the place from which he fell; others of us may hold that by religion man in his ascent is aided toward the place where he ought to be; but in either case religion is normal in the very best sense.

A second preliminary remark. Religion is youthful. There is a time in life for dolls and make-believe. There is a time in life for hero-worship. There is a time for that awkward ungainly period when the boy is becoming a man, and when his voice is likely at any moment to miss-cue and slip without warning from a growling, lion-like bass to a squeaky, piping treble. [story] And just as truly there is a time in life for religion, and youth is the time.

A third preliminary remark. Religion is necessary. "Knowledge is power," says the old proverb. Yes, and so is dynamite, and both are dangerous. "Knowledge is virtue," says Socrates. But we must have a very unusual definition of knowledge to accept his statement without a grain of salt, for we all realize that often we know the better and do the worse. All their knowledge, if knowledge is their all, does not restrain medical students from vice.

We who have come to maturity, or may even have passed the meridian of life, know that an anchorage is necessary even though the storms of passion may be largely stilled. And if it is easier than it once was to stay in the right paths, let us not deceive ourselves by mistaking weariness for virtue. The man of 40 or 50 or 60 needs the anchorage of a religious life. How much more, then, does the youth need religion, with appetites, desires, temptations at their maximum, with discretion in its infancy, wisdom but partly developed, strength of character only half-grown? If middle age needs religion, and it does, there is no safety for youth without it.

If then religion is normal and youthful and necessary, no program of education which omits religion can with reason claim to be even reasonably adequate.

One recognizes, of course, the fact that the educational institution proper can have only a part of the great work of developing the religious life. The first of this work, and the best of it, should have been done in the home before even the kindergarten and the primary school have their chance to make or mar the character of the child. From cradle-roll to the classes where senile age looks through the sunset of life and sees the gates ajar, the Bible school should be doing its work of religious teaching and religious training—indeed it should be doing a vastly better work than it has ever yet done. Through the Christian Endeavor or other similar young people's societies, and in various other ways the church should be ministering directly to the religious education of its own young people and of those young people who are not within the pales of the church, but for whom in so-called Christian America the church should certainly be responsible. Even in its regular meetings for worship that church which is not through pulpit and choir and every other part of its service ministering to genuine religious education is falling short of its privilege and its duty. But our discussion has to do with the place of religion in our program as educational institutions.

There is not time in the presentation of this subject for the discussion of religion in connection with the public schools, high schools, state colleges and state universities. The difficulty of the maintenance of an adequate program of religious education in schools of this sort will readily be recognized. Our public educational institutions, maintained by the taxation alike of Jew and

Gentile, Protestant and Catholic, Liberal and Conservative, Quaker and KKK, Modernist and Fundamentalist—these public schools of ours present great difficulties for the carrying out of any adequate religious program. It seems to be conceded by many if not by most educators that in our public school system religion is, if it finds a place, an extra, a side-issue, a thing carried on, if it is carried on, by a splendid group of men and women in the Y.M. and Y.W., in church, in Sunday School, etc., in the town where the educational institution is located, and by other means not under direct control of the educational institution itself. All honor to the splendid men and women, older and younger, who are in so many places doing their great work for religion in the face of such difficulties and under such handicaps.

But I am speaking from the standpoint of the independent college, which is usually a denominational college, and whose chief reason for existence I take to be the religious reason. The small denominational college has many disadvantages and serious limitations, but it has some great advantages which the great school cannot have, and is free of some of the handicaps which are inevitably incident to the great school.

What should be, then, the place of religion in the small college, the independent college, the denominational college, the Christian college?

First of all, it seems to me that religion should be all pervasive in schools such as those from which most of us have come. The teaching of science, the teaching of history, the teaching of mathematics, and of all the other things in our curriculum, should be religious in the best sense. The man who teaches science irreverently and so as to wreck the faith of his students is as criminal as the man who rocks the boat or the one who throws children overboard to make them good swimmers. It may make good swimmers of some, but it drowns others. There is a better way to teach swimming without so large a percentage of fatality. The man who cannot teach science reverently ought never to be allowed on the faculty of a Christian college. The man who cannot see God in history belongs in the home for the blind, not in the faculty of a Christian college.

If you gather that I mean that the faculty of such an institution as yours and mine should be religious, definitely and positively and reverently Christian, you have understood exactly what

I mean. A man cannot teach intellectual things best without some touch with Him who is Infinite Wisdom. Even the man who would teach physical training successfully is in desperate need of knowledge, not only of the physical organism of body and nerve and brain, but of intellect, emotion, will, and character. The best teacher of the body and the best teacher of the mind need also a knowledge of the soul. How much more does the teacher of religion need himself to be deeply religious. It is still true of religion as of character that it is far more frequently caught than taught.

In addition to this pervasive religious atmosphere which ought to be in every classroom and on the athletic field as well as in the chapel service, there is a place for definite courses in religious education.

In the judgment of the speaker there should be some requirement in religious education as a requisite for graduation. Of course, religion cannot be forced, but if a young man is not entitled to graduation without a certain knowledge of history, of science, of mathematics, of foreign language, it seems to the speaker that no student should graduate from a Christian college who has not taken some work in course in the line of religious education.

In addition to required work in course in which there should doubtless be room for a fairly wide selection, there should be optional work offered of a fairly extensive character. It would seem that even the smaller Christian college might well offer three courses of a predominately historical character, one dealing with Old Testament history, one with New Testament history, and one with the history of Christianity since New Testament times. In addition to this historical minimum, there should be at least three other courses of a more definitely biblical and devotional type. One should deal with the religious literature of the Old Testament; one should be devoted to the teachings of Jesus; and one to the further development of the Christian ideals in the other New Testament writings.

There is, of course, no limit to the amount of work that might be offered if we had student bodies, faculties, and financial resources to justify it. We are working in colleges, however, rather than in theological seminaries or training schools for Christian workers, and with all the things that might be offered the suggested courses as a minimum serve at least as a basis for expansion.

In addition to the courses in religious education and biblical work as such, the Christian college should make its various departments minister more or less directly to the Christian ideal. The relation of numerous other subjects to the religious life will readily be seen. Philosophy, ethics, and various other subjects lend themselves readily to the teaching of religion, not in a forced but in a perfectly natural way. And, as already stated, the Christian ideal and reverence therefore should permeate all our teaching.

In the extra-curricular activities of schools such as ours there is room for the definite advancement of Christian ideals. Most of these activities will probably be carried on in connection with the work of the Christian association. In Bible study classes, mission study class, discussion groups, etc., much can be done to stimulate and build up the Christian life of an institution. We might pause in passing to acknowledge the need of wise leadership in connection with the freedom of discussion in such groups which often are tremendously powerful for good but which if under the wrong kind of leadership sometimes do less good than they ought, and may even do more harm than good.

It is often necessary to emphasize among students the fact that college is not merely a place of preparation for life, but a place where life is actually being lived. It is therefore important not only that the student *study* religion, but that he *practice* it. The practice of religion is as essential to religious life as proper exercise and nutrition are to the physical life.

And by the practice of religion I refer not primarily to the observance of the requirements of the church, important as they are. There is an ever-present danger of the divorce of religious experience and religious ritual from actual religious life possible. On the negative side this will mean what Sam Jones called "quitting your meanness." On the positive side it will mean the doing of definite good.

And our program should lay emphasis not only on the *study* of religion and the *practice* of religion, but also definitely on the *propagation* of religion. He who looks upon Christianity merely as a spiritual fire-escape has not understood Christ, nor His religion. Every religious life should be propagating itself, and our students should constantly see the importance of the propagation of religion.

The most immediate opportunity is among their own school mates. It is hard for a man to believe that he has influence over another, but he has, and he ought to exercise it. [Story] The second place where every student should propagate Christianity is in his own home community. Our colleges have been criticized, sometimes unjustly, but it is to be feared, sometimes justly, because our students have gone back to their home communities and have not been able to fit into the work of the church from which they came. A genuine Christian college man or woman should be unusually adaptable.

And our religious program cannot be complete unless we emphasize the propagation of Christianity in other lands. Three-fourths of those who hear the call to sacrificial service hear it before the close of their high school years; the rest must get it during their college days or it is for ever too late. It must continue to be true that the most of our missionaries and the best of our missionaries come from our Christian colleges, where they have seen the heavenly vision and learned and prepared themselves to be obedient.

In conclusion I should say that the aim of our religious program should be to aid our students to a saving knowledge of Jesus Christ as personal Savior and Lord; to a dedication of life to the advancement of His Kingdom in the earth; to the development of spiritual knowledge and power as the body and mind develop, "till we all come to the perfect man, to the measure of the stature of the fulness of Christ."

A LAYMAN'S LOOK AT THE LAW

(Synopsis of an address given before the Oregon State Bar Association at Bend, Oregon, September 30, 1927.)

It seems a bit strange that I should be asked to talk to you. Possibly it was with some such thought as was expressed when one of our church leaders made an impassioned speech on a matter with which he was not at all conversant, and one of our leaders remarked, "How eloquent a man can be when he is not hampered by facts and information." Surely my knowledge of the law will not hamper me much in what I have to say.

But in another way it does not seem so strange that I should be asked to speak to the lawyers when I think how many kinds of folks know and are ready to tell me how to run my job. The butcher, the baker, the candle-stick maker, the grocer, the doctor, the ditch digger—yes, and some lawyers are ready to help me, and I get some good suggestions from some of them too.

Most of you have read Ernest Seton Thompson's book, *Wild Animals I Have Known*. It has been my privilege in the last few years to travel much, and I have been in forty of the forty-eight states during that time. I have met many lawyers, and perhaps I could write a book about certain lawyers I have known. I shall never do that, but I do want to tell you about one lawyer I have met and one judge of whom I know. This lawyer breaks the law; and this judge drinks bootleg whiskey.

Now I do not want to be narrow minded. I heard recently of a man so narrow minded that a mosquito could stand on the bridge of his nose and kick him in both eyes at once. I do not want to be narrow minded, but I hope I shall never be so broad minded that a bootlegger's auto of moonshine whiskey can go tearing lawlessly through, smearing with its muddy wheels the constitution and laws of the United States and of the state of Oregon, which you are every one sworn to uphold, dragging the flag of my country through the mud of lawlessness, without my protest. It is as fitting for a teacher to pervert the truth, for a minister to lead his flock into vice and wickedness, or for a physician to sow the germs of pestilence in his community, as for a lawyer to violate the law, which he is sworn to uphold. You claim to be patriots, and some of you may consider yourselves "One Hundred Per Cent Americans." I do not know exactly what 100% American is, though recently a man gave a suggestion when he stepped from a meeting where Jews, Catholics, Negroes, and foreigners had all been denounced, with the remark, "I'm a 200% American, I hate everybody." But whatever a 100% American is it is my conviction that when a man says he is a 100% American while at the same time he violates his country's laws and defies its constitution, he is showing what a long eared, mouse colored ass a man can be when he throws away everything from his eyebrows up. He is saying to the European Red, "Come over and help me tear down the temple of the constitution. I am doing my best but I need your assistance." So far as I remember, none of you has asked me for my opinion, but you can have it without asking—when a bootlegger sells a bottle of moonshine to a lawyer that bootlegger should go to prison; and in the cell next to his, but with a longer sentence should be the lawyer, I care not how high he holds his head, who committed the graver offense of buying that booze—for the lawyer knew so much better. "Unto whom much is given of him shall much be required." And as for my opinion of the *judge* who will violate the law—well, I quit that sort of language when I became a Christian—I'll just turn him over to Billy Sunday, who does not share some of my scruples as to what words may properly be used.

Well, that's my first point, if I never make another. A lawyer should obey the law. We shall have gone far when all the folks with the best education and opportunities accept, both in theory and practice, the idea that laws are to be obeyed, not merely enforced.

When I was a young man I wanted to be a lawyer. But I somehow developed an antipathy to law, medicine and undertaking—all thrive, as it seemed to me then, on the misfortunes of others. I thought an undertaker came around only when somebody was dead—now I know he sometimes comes around when he merely expects that somebody is going to die. I thought doctors were only useful when somebody was sick—now I know that the whole reputable part of the medical profession is at work on the greater task of preventing and eradicating disease. I used to think that lawyers had to do only with violation of law—the prosecutor to bring the criminal to justice, if possible; and the attorney for the defense to help the criminal to escape the consequence and enjoy the fruits of his crime, if possible. Well, there may be, I suspect there is, more truth in that than there ought to be. There is enough truth to give force to the epigram when the caustic critic of our present system says, "Our courts have ceased to be places where justice is judiciously dispensed, and have become places where justice is judicially dispensed with."

I wish all lawyers were as vitally interested in teaching the ways of obedience to law as the good physician is in teaching healthful living; as earnest to abolish lawlessness as the reputable part of the medical profession is in stamping out yellow-fever, cholera, the black plague, the red death.

I wish we could reform our whole court procedure, which so protects the possible innocent as to give the criminal, especially the wealthy criminal, more than an even chance to escape the consequences of his crime. But it may be that this is too much to hope; and if such a reform comes it seems to me it must come from within, not from without. But in the matter of teaching obedience to law almost no change in system is necessary, no new enactments, no breaking of iron bound traditions, no giving of yourself into the hands of your enemy. In my judgment the lawyers of Oregon could do more than any other class in the way of direct action toward the ending of our widely advertised and all too real "reign of lawlessness."

This then is my second suggestion. In addition to wholehearted and unvarying obedience to law, let the lawyer *teach* obedience to law.

We are all concerned over this "reign of lawlessness," and we should all like to see the end that we might no longer be shamed by the fact that a single American city has more homicides in a year than a European country three times its population has in a decade. We think that reform of our court proceedings would help. We think that more vigor on the part of our enforcement officials would aid. We are sure that more severity toward law breakers, and less maudlin sentiment on the part of our "sobsisters" of both sexes would be to our advantage. But none of these, nor all of them combined, will end the lawlessness which so many influences in addition to those suggested have brought upon us.

More and more I am impressed as the years pass with that aphorism, "If the answer is easy, it's wrong."

Slavery had fastened itself upon America very firmly in the two and a half centuries that it had existed here. The emancipation proclamation of Lincoln set the slaves free so far as an executive order could do it. But these constituted the easy answer, and the answer that was wrong, because inadequate; the solution of the problem of human slavery is not so easy as this.

The problem of the use of intoxicants loomed large in the thinking of many of our best people for decades in my own memory. When I was a boy I would have been sure that if the use of intoxicating liquors as a beverage were forbidden by United States law, and still more, if prohibition were written into the

United States Constitution that the problem of intemperance would be solved. But this again constituted the relatively easy answer that was wrong in that it was inadequate. We know that the problem of intemperance is not settled yet. Much more must yet be done.

War has threatened the world since the dawn of history, and now stands insolently before civilization saying, "You must destroy me or I shall destroy you." We may have hoped that arbitration treaties would solve the question, or that a world court would settle, or that a league of nations would make war impossible. I believe we will all agree now that these things constitute the easy answer which is wrong because inadequate.

And no easy answer to our problem of lawlessness can constitute a real solution. To make a nation of law-abiding citizens we must begin at the bottom, the home, the school, the church, and other great influences which mold the oncoming generation must all work, and all work together. But in my judgment the legal profession is a great and too largely unutilized force in the development of a law-abiding citizenry. I wish this bar association would undertake, through every means possible, and especially through the schools, both public and private, to teach to the coming generation the fundamental things of morals and obedience to law.

Notes to Chapter III

1. University of Oregon Collection (UOC).
2. Family Papers (FP).
3. (FP).
4. (FP).
5. (FP).
6. (FP).
7. Shambaugh Library (SL).
8. (SL).
9. (SL).
10. (SL).
11. (SL).
12. (SL).
13. (FP).
14. (FP).
15. (UOC).
16. (FP).

CHAPTER
IV | The
Agony
1931-1947

LEVI T. PENNINGTON wrote many letters in which he expressed great stress and anguish over two events directly affecting Oregon Yearly Meeting and Pacific College: the withdrawal of Oregon Yearly Meeting from the Five Years Meeting (1926), and the release of Emmett Gulley from the presidency of Pacific College (1947). These events resulted in a long and serious alienation of Pennington from many Oregon Friends—an alienation in part intellectual, because it concerned both perception of situation and interpretation of church polity; in part religious conviction because it involved adherence to firmly held views; and finally, it was social because it involved Pennington's friendship and tested the strength of his influence. His reaction to these events significantly reveal facets of LTP's character.

Any life, especially a long, active life of public significance, can only be understood as it moves before its various and changing backgrounds. Such a life, like that of character in drama, is revealed slowly by piecing together small actions and scenes which finally round out the life drama. Sometimes these are too elusive to construct even into a satisfactory, hypothetical pattern, and in such instances the effort results in an incomplete or distorted image of a life. The classic example of the many Shakespeare biographies is a warning to anyone who becomes involved in the complexity of reconstructing another's life and actions, for who has yet woven the thousands of words and phrases, the isolated scraps of information, into the play that was Shakespeare's life? The cue to be taken from this in reconstructing Pennington's life is to show some of his representative positions and reasoning with the warning, "Here are some ideas which this man held that may convey some insights for better understanding his actions."

Pennington's angry response to these situations can only be appreciated when it is realized that after devoting the major portion of his career to Oregon Yearly Meeting and Pacific College, anything of significance that happened to either organization in a sense happened to him. Both were his life, his own identity, made more personal because he had formulated certain notions about how each should function. However, his personal involvement was deeper than this suggests, for throughout his life he had also been a part of the Five Years Meeting. He was schooled at Earlham College, where he had become acquainted with Five Years Meeting leaders; later he served as one of its clerks; he also gave long service to several of its committees including the executive committee, and finally he became one of its administrators. Thus the Five Years Meeting like Oregon Yearly Meeting and Pacific College was also a part of his personal identity. To withdraw from them was unthinkable; in fact no indication remains that he contemplated any withdrawal even within his most distressed period.

In similar fashion LTP was emotionally involved in the life and career of Emmett Gulley. Gulley was one of his students at Pacific. He too was large and strong, a competitive athlete, mirroring in part LTP's college career and aspirations. He became a trusted and respected friend, Pennington's choice to succeed him as president of the college. Because Pennington was sensitive to the trends within the college following his retirement, he reacted strongly to actions of the trustees, perhaps overreacted when he believed any friend was treated unjustly by the college.

While these events loomed large in his memory during this troubled era of the late 1940s, some of his emotional explosiveness arose from other previous actions of the Yearly Meeting. Among them was the boundary problem between Oregon and Indiana Yearly Meetings involving the state of Washington, in 1918 and 1919. His high regard for the American Friends Service Committee and its work prompted strong reaction when it was condemned by the Yearly Meeting following World War I. In essence, these events appear to have joined together in his thinking in the late

1940s and he began to feel the necessity for speaking out against what he felt to be a utilitarian course of action by the Yearly Meeting dating from the pre-1920s. Finally his "sense of injured merit" prompted an address before the Meeting of Ministry and Oversight of Oregon Yearly Meeting, August 16, 1950, on the topic, "Shall We Do Evil that Good May Come?"

His 3,000-word address was highly generalized. The discussion was random, without an adequate summary of actions to constitute an intellectual appeal to the audience. Rather, it depended upon the memories of the listeners, even though some of these events had taken place a quarter century earlier. It seems safe to assume that in any church business meeting, few would have accurate knowledge of actions so long in the past; therefore, a careful summary of grievances might have elicited sympathy for his message. In summary, it consisted of urging those present to make all decisions in the light of honest judgments, not by following the philosophy of "the end justifies the means." Its lack of logical organization combined with its general attack suggests that it was conceived as an emotional response. As such it contrasts sharply with his well-developed presentations seeking appeal through artful persuasion.

His courage in criticizing past actions is admirable, for it stemmed from conviction, but its emotional involvement indicates that frustration had increased until the central issues were blurred. These conclusions become inevitable from an analysis of the address; however, the character of the man behind it is not opened like a book; rather it remains hidden, even distorted, by the outward appearance.

If the address seems misplaced at the time it was given, it does provide a window for seeing an important aspect of his character: his genuine honesty. This quality is revealed by comparing his address with letters of the same period in which he discussed the same subject. These letters to friends and to members of his own family with whom he was always open and frank including his daughter Mary, his cousin Mary White, a missionary to Jamaica, his former classmate and debate partner, Homer L. Morris, and Lloyd Cressman were only slightly less reserved than in his address. In fact, many paragraphs from them could be substituted for paragraphs in the address without changing either its tone or verbal content. This testifies to the integrity and openness of Pennington's character.

He was not perfidious for he spoke his mind, perhaps more frankly than wisdom might sometimes dictate, perhaps with verbal sharpness that he later regretted, but with the strength of conviction. This quality of the early Quakers under Fox became their trademark. They openly spoke their convictions about war, slavery, treatment of prisoners, and social behavior before the magistrates, even though it incurred great physical danger. While seventeenth century bluntness should not be used to justify a disregard for contemporary tactfulness, allowance must be made in mature dialogue for the expression of honest feeling and judgment by accepting it objectively. Pennington often opposed the status quo, and he seemed undaunted when espousing a cause that proved unpopular, because its popularity was not the criteria for evaluating its worthiness; rather, he asked if it were biblical, if it were right, and if it were Quakerly.

Pennington was more general in discussing the boundary problem between the two yearly meetings than the other problems. This situation, as reconstructed from the official minutes, can be summarized as follows: The 1918 *Minutes* records the text of a communication from the Executive Committee of the Five Years Meeting to OYM on behalf of the Evangelistic Committee of Indiana Yearly Meeting which closes with the following paragraph:

> We therefore hope that Oregon Yearly Meeting will not carry on or promote Evangelistic or Pastoral work within the limits of the district belonging to Indiana Yearly Meeting, except in the fullest co-operation with the Evangelistic Committee of Indiana Yearly Meeting.[1]

In response to this communication the Representatives met and reported to the Yearly Meeting, "We heartily and unanimously concur in the suggestion presented to the Yearly Meeting by the Executive Committee of the Five Years Meeting, concerning the work of Oregon Yearly Meeting in the limits of Puget Sound Quarterly Meeting."[2] Acting upon this recommendation, the Nominating Committee appointed four persons to work with the Evangelistic Board of OYM and the Executive Committee of the Five Years Meeting.[3]

The joint committee reported its recommendations to the 1919 Yearly Meeting: (1) that a boundary be established in the state of Washington between the two yearly meetings, and that the meetings in Tacoma and Entiat be transferred to Oregon Yearly Meeting. This permitted the Friends churches in Seattle and Everett to remain with Indiana Yearly Meeting, and in effect excluded this area of Puget Sound from development by Oregon Yearly Meeting.

Pennington's charge was that Oregon Yearly Meeting had, subsequent to this agreement, opened a church in the Seattle area, simply because it was convenient to do so. However, by the time of the address in 1950, all of the Puget Sound meetings formerly under Indiana had joined with Oregon. Arthur Roberts, who became pastor of the Everett church in 1944, gave leadership to the transfer of this meeting, although final action was not complete until later, under John Frazier. Memorial Church in Seattle, established in 1905 under the authority of Winchester Quarterly Meeting of Indiana, survived several reverses and finally emerged under the leadership of Milo Ross, who began his work there in 1949 by building a badly needed church building. Although the meeting had requested to unite with Oregon Yearly Meeting in 1947, this was not made final until June 1949 (*A Garden of the Lord*, pp. 256-258). Because this difficulty between the two yearly meetings had been resolved, it is doubtful if any purpose was served by including this problem in the address. It undoubtedly deepened the gulf between Pennington and the Yearly Meeting leaders without accomplishing an act of leadership.

Only five years before the address, Oregon Yearly Meeting had passed an act of contrition in an attempt to atone for the past error. The Evangelistic and Church Extension Board sent a communication to the Yearly Meeting which closed with the following statements:

> According to available records of Oregon and Indiana Yearly Meetings it is evident that Oregon Yearly Meeting has violated an agreement entered into by both Yearly Meetings relative to territorial boundaries in the state of Washington.

> In view of this we recommend that Oregon Yearly Meeting direct a communication to Indiana Yearly Meeting, confessing the wrong of

our actions in violating this agreement and that we humbly ask their forgiveness.

The recommendation was approved.[4]

A more serious concern to Pennington was the withdrawal of Oregon Yearly Meeting from the Five Years Meeting in June 1926. This culminated a struggle which began seriously in 1919 when dissatisfaction with the Five Years Meeting came before the Yearly Meeting in its annual session as resolutions from two bodies: one an action from an unofficial group of representatives of the Yearly Meeting in Portland May 7, 1919, and the other a resolution drawn up by Scotts Mills Monthly Meeting May 14, 1919. It was endorsed by the Salem Quarterly Meeting three days later.

These actions officially opened the subject of withdrawal, resulting in a long and frequently bitter struggle between those who saw wisdom in remaining in the larger church body and those who were equally determined to separate from it. The story of the struggle between 1919 and the final action in 1926 is very complex; too much of its history lies outside official actions and minutes for piecing together into a complete account, but the main issues are clear from the official record upon which this summary is based.

In an effort not to distort by summary, the complete texts of the original, signed copies of both the Portland Conference and the Scotts Mills Meeting are given. These actions remain historically important because through them the subject of Oregon Yearly Meeting's withdrawal from the Five Years Meeting officially came to the floor of the Yearly Meeting session, and because with only slight modification, these positions remained as the basic dissatisfactions with the Five Years Meeting throughout the difficult years of decision. They are presented because they appear to represent the perception of those who favored seceding only against which Pennington's perceptions can be meaningful.

The minutes of the Portland Conference reads:

By invitation a number of members of the Friends Church met at the First Friends Church Portland May 7/1919 to council together in matters pertaining to the church.

The following Friends were invited:

From Boise Valley - T.C. Perisho, E.G. Pearson, Wm. Street, Linn Heston, C.I. Whitlock, and Marion Shattuck.

Salem - C.A. Hadley, I.G. Lee, Mrs. Lee, Fred Harris, Blaine Bronner, H.E. Pemberton, Anna B. Miles and Matilda Minthorn.

Newberg - Levi T. Pennington, Aaron Bray, Fred Carter, Carl Miller, Wm. Allen, Lewis Russel and Marietta Lewis. (Harlan G. Smith written in).

Portland - F.M. George, H.L. Cox, Laurana Terrell, J.S. Fox, Effie Tamplin, Lewis I. Hadley, O.J. Sherman and Lydia C. Gardner.

All were present but H.E. Pemberton of South Salem.

The meeting was opened with singing and prayer. H.L. Cox was chosen chairman and Anna B. Miles secretary.

The subject that claimed the attention of the meeting was the attitude of some of the members of Oregon Yearly Meeting towards the Five Years Meeting.

A great deal of dissatisfaction was expressed in regard to the different Boards of the Five Years Meeting, especially the Board of Publication and the Bible School Board.

At 12:25 the meeting adjourned until 2:00 P.M.

At 2:00 P.M. the conference convened as per adjournment, opened with a song and prayer service.

A discussion on the subject of the morning session continued; the different pastors were called upon to give the attitude of their meetings toward the two boards mentioned.

On motion a committee was appointed to frame a resolution and present it to this meeting. Lemuel Heston, Aaron Bray, Gurney Lee, Laurana M. Terrell, (and by virtue of his office) Homer Cox, shall constitute this committee, and they are requested to report at 5:30. A recess was taken until that hour.

At 5:30, or soon after, the meeting convened and the following resolution was presented.

Whereas: The Uniform Discipline refers to the letter of George Fox to the Governor of Barbadoes in 1671, and to the Declaration of Faith, issued by the Richmond Conference in 1887, as standard beliefs of the church:

And whereas: Oregon Yearly Meeting at the time it adopted the Uniform Discipline considered these standard declarations as a part of the beliefs of the church, and binding upon our membership:

And whereas: Said Board of Publication is publishing the American Friend, and the Bible School Board is publishing various Bible School periodicals and papers:

Therefore: Be it resolved by Oregon Yearly Meeting of Friends in regular session assembled, that it is the sense of this meeting that in order to secure and maintain the full moral and financial support of the above mentioned Yearly Meeting, the Boards heretofore mentioned must publish only those utterances in harmony with the doctrinal standards heretofore mentioned.

Be it further resolved: That the members of this meeting who are also members of the Board of Publication, and the Bible School Board of the Five Years Meeting, are hereby directed and required to use all their influence and authority to carry out the provisions of the foregoing resolution.

Be it resolved: The members of this meeting who are members of the two Boards heretofore mentioned, are hereby directed and required to report to this meeting next year their action in this matter.

The resolution was adopted.

By consent, the committee on resolutions was continued to form a resolution with regard to the attitude of Oregon Yearly Meeting toward the Five Years Meeting in reference to Missionary Work.

(signed) Homer L. Cox, Chairman[5]

This resolution was adopted by the Yearly Meeting.[6] The resolution concerning missionary work, although drawn up and signed by members of the committee, was modified before adoption in the following statement:

Resolved: That while appreciating the many problems which would naturally come to such Boards, and sincerely wishing to be helpful in our criticism of the same, we feel that in order to give the American Friends Board the fullest cooperation of this yearly meeting in our united efforts to fulfill the command of the Lord, 'Go into all the world and preach the gospel to every creature,' that it would be well to have inserted in the application blank for use of candidates for the field some question which would help the Board to ascertain whether or not the applicant had definitely sought and received the baptism with the Holy Ghost, which our branch of His church believes to be essential to carrying out the command of our Master referred to above.[7]

The resolution drafted by the Scotts Mills Monthly Meeting raised objections in two of the areas covered by the Portland Conference: official publications and missionary work. Their resolution was more pointed in its accusations against the Five Years Meeting than that issued in Portland, and its objections were voiced in more alarming language, thereby demonstrating the manner by which emotions began to surface. It further demonstrates that differences existed within the perception of how to resolve disagreement. Following is the text of the original, signed copy of the Scotts Mills meeting:

> At a called meeting of Scotts Mills Monthly Meeting, held 5th Month 14th 1919, the following resolution was read and unanimously adopted and the following committee was appointed to see to the presentation of the same to the Quarterly Meeting, the same also to be forwarded to Yearly Meeting, W.L. Taylor, Jno. S. Richie, and E.W. Coulson.

> The following is the resolution adopted: - Having observed, with exceeding regret, that the Five Years Meeting of Friends, established and existing solely by the concurrent action and suffrage of the Majority of the American Yearly Meetings, has habitually and with increasing boldness, exceeded the power and authority conferred upon it at the time of its organization, we desire at this time to speak with special reference to the Official Literature and Publications and concerning its Missionary Board.

> We have been alarmed at the independent spirit manifested in publishing that which is directly Contrary to the Quaker Doctrine Concerning the word of God and Man's Salvation, and declining to publish Orthodox Refutation of the same.

> We have again been alarmed at the attitude taken by the Missionary Board in its apparent attempt to regulate the appointments to Missionary Fields from those who are in sympathy with their beliefs. While not claiming that each member of the Five Years' Missionary Board believes in or is in sympathy with Destructive Higher Criticism—so called—we do know that the dominating power in it is in sympathy with this fearful heresy.

> Knowing these things, and feeling that we can no longer conscientiously give our Moral or Financial support to the Five Years Meeting and its various Boards, we propose to Oregon Yearly Meeting that we withdraw entirely from that Organization.

> Signed on behalf of the Scotts Mills Monthly Meeting

> E.W. Coulson, Clerk
> Lila L. Brougher, Ass't Clerk

Adopted by the Salem Quarterly Meeting held at Rosedale, 5th Mo. 17th, 1919.

Myrtle M. Russell, Presiding Clerk
Anna B. Miles, Recording Clerk for the day[8]

The Yearly Meeting Representatives submitted this resolution to the Yearly Meeting with the recommendation that it be submitted to the quarterly meetings for their vote during the following year, and the results reported to the next Yearly Meeting. This recommendation was approved by the Yearly Meeting session.[9]

The next step toward withdrawal was taken in the 1920 sessions, following the reports from the quarterly meetings. Three voted against and four voted for withdrawal; however, the report from the Boise Valley Quarterly Meeting contained a resolution similar to those a year earlier from Portland and Scotts Mills, but with a new dimension. It included a statement, "It is therefore understood that if these conditions are not remedied by the next Five Years Meeting in the re-organization of its various Boards, Oregon Yearly Meeting will feel at liberty to withdraw should it so elect." The complete resolution was adopted by the Yearly Meeting and it became the document forwarded to the General Secretary of the Five Years Meeting.

A commentary on Pennington's behavior as presiding clerk is preserved by the next item of business in the same session, "The meeting gave a vote of appreciation to the presiding clerk for the fair manner in which he conducted the business of the afternoon."[10]

By Yearly Meeting time in 1924 events began to point toward a more conservative turn in Oregon Yearly Meeting. Perhaps the first evidence of this was the replacement of Pennington as presiding clerk of the Yearly Meeting by Edward Mott, which ended a ten-year tenure in this leadership role. This action can be interpreted as dissatisfaction with Pennington's influence in stressing the humanitarian concern of Friends in favor of Edward Mott who was not thus identified.

At the opening of the Yearly Meeting sessions, the superintendent, L. Clarkson Hinshaw, in making his report sounded a conciliatory note toward the Five Years Meeting when he said, "The action of the Five Years Meeting during its recent session in approving and endorsing the Historic Doctrines of the church involved all in that respect, that this or any other Yearly Meeting has ever asked for, and should end all controversy as to the doctrinal basis of our united work."[11] However, on the following day the Ministerial Association requested the Yearly Meeting to take positive action toward enforcing a reformation within the boards and staffs of the Five Years Meeting. This action resulted in a resolution by the Yearly Meeting to allow two years for this to be accomplished. The closing paragraph of this resolution stated:

> Therefore, it is the conviction of Oregon Yearly Meeting at this time, that the Executive and Publication Board of the Five Years Meeting assume this responsibility at once; and it is hereby understood that if the policies of the different boards are not reshaped as to conform to and consistently sustain the standards that have been approved and endorsed by the authority of the Five Years Meeting by the convening of Oregon Yearly Meeting in the year 1926, this Yearly Meeting will not consider itself any longer an organic part of the Five Years Meeting; and that a judicious committee be appointed by the Yearly Meeting to be nominated by the representative body, to have this matter in charge and report its findings to the Yearly Meeting at its first session in 1926.[12]

The representatives nominated a committee of twelve members with five alternates; the report was adopted and the committee was instructed to report in the first session of the Yearly Meeting in 1926. Levi Pennington was among those named to the committee.

The first meeting of the committee was held April 11, 1926, at the Newberg Friends Church. Both L. Clarkson Hinshaw and Robert Dann declined to chair the committee, and finally Raymond S. Holding agreed to serve as chairman. The minutes and transcript of the committee meetings show that a general discussion was held in the first meeting to consider the consequences both of remaining in the Five Years Meeting and withdrawing from it. An attempt was also made to clarify the issues involved in the dissatisfaction of Oregon Yearly Meeting with the Five Years Meeting. Much more was said in favor of remaining than of withdrawing, although the committee concluded by the end of the meeting that little new had been added to the thinking of either side.

The second meeting was held at the same location, April 25. As this meeting progressed the group became more sharply divided, although both sides demonstrated a concern for more wisdom in order to judge what was best for the entire Friends movement. Still no conclusion was reached.

In the third session held May 2 in Salem, the committee decided to hear a statement from two of its members, one favoring withdrawal from the Five Years Meeting and the other supporting the opposing view. Mrs. B.C. Miles called the meeting to order, but because I. Gurney Lee was not present to speak in favor of withdrawal this address was given by Carl F. Miller. The summary of his address contained in the minutes is rather brief and can be fairly represented by four of its most substantiative paragraphs:

> The attitude of the committee whose report we have heard and are considering is that Oregon Yearly Meeting in 1924 decided that the Five Years Meeting leaders are not orthodox. It was our understanding that we were to report whether that leadership has been changed or not since 1924.
>
> Matters of doctrinal belief are the basis of the difficulty as it has come before the committee.
>
> I have been asked to tell the advantages of Oregon being outside the Five Years Meeting. Nobody can tell until we try. I don't want to be personal. We'll have problems either way. We need a central organization, I am sure of that.
>
> Not all the Five Years Meeting leaders are unsound . . . . But in my judgment some of our leaders would have done better if they had done as . . . did when the storm was centered about him. He resigned. [13]

Levi T. Pennington was asked to speak in favor of remaining within the Five Years Meeting. His address appears to be complete in the minutes even though it is listed as "Summary of Speech of Levi T. Pennington." In this form it is nearly 3,000 words. [14] This address to the committee is his answer to the whole area of criticism and reasoning advanced within the Yearly Meeting by those who sought to withdraw from the larger body of Friends. As such it is a definitive statement of his position and has to be read without abridgment, even though it is long, for only then will his position be clear as he sought to answer the resolutions and reports of the previous Yearly Meeting sessions. Its striking qualities are its logical, clear, yet forceful presentation combined with its tone of calm objectivity. It may be one of his most articulate arguments remaining in print.

The 1926 Yearly Meeting sessions began June 10, and the action to withdraw became the business of Minute 11. If emotions were present in this session, they are not reflected in the record of the meeting. Before action was taken, a brief history of the relation of Oregon Yearly Meeting to the Uniform Discipline and subsequent uneasiness over its doctrinal position was presented, beginning with the General Conference of Yearly Meetings held in Indianapolis, Indiana, in 1897, prior to the organization of the Five Years Meeting. This summary outlined the various actions taken in an effort to bring the officers of the Five Years Meeting into a commitment to the doctrinal statement deemed necessary by Oregon Yearly Meeting and thereby served to give perspective to the proposed recommendation to withdraw. Despite Pennington's substitute motion to continue as a part of the larger body, action to withdraw prevailed.

If one places this entire chapter of Oregon Yearly Meeting in perspective as a part of Quaker history, the withdrawal is reduced to a lesser issue. Traditionally, the Quaker movement had existed as independent yearly meetings which recognized each other by epistles of greeting and by goodwill extended by visiting delegates. However, the positive response to the first General Conference of Yearly Meetings in 1887 led to the decision to hold similar conferences of the American yearly meetings every five years. In 1897 an even closer union of the yearly meetings appeared advisable, and twelve yearly meetings which had approved the Uniform Discipline, drawn up by this cooperative effort, became the Five Years Meeting. The Oregon debate centered upon two considerations: (1) can we as a Yearly Meeting accomplish more by becoming independent, and (2) can we continue to cooperate with and support a movement whose religious education literature and missionary effort fail to emphasize those beliefs and practices which we believe are necessary? Pennington and a few leaders believed that breaking from the larger body of Friends would weaken the capabilities of Oregon Yearly Meeting; they did not accept the assumption and charge that some of the leaders in the Five Years Meeting were not orthodox. More specifically, LTP felt that those fighting for withdrawal had resorted to attacking the leaders rather than the issues.

Historically, there was nothing sacrosanct about a yearly meeting belonging to an organic union of yearly meetings beyond commitments that tied them together. Pennington recognized this, but his immediate indignation was aroused by the procedural manner in which the voting was conducted by the presiding clerk in determining the will of the Yearly Meeting.

As President Pennington prepared to retire in 1941, it was necessary to select his successor. The College Board appointed Emmett W. Gulley, who was Pennington's choice and whose background of experience and training gave credibility to his appointment. In commending him to the Yearly Meeting in his final college report in 1941, Pennington reminded his listeners that Gulley was a product of Pacific College having graduated from it in the class of 1917 after attending the college 1912-1914 and 1915-1917. Following his graduation he attended the Hartford Theological Seminary School of Missions for one year followed by service as a Friends missionary in Mexico for five years. Upon returning from this assignment he studied for another year in the T. Wistar Brown Graduate School of Haverford College, from which he received his master's degree. He then became the field secretary of New York Yearly Meeting of Friends, a post he held for four years until his appointment to the faculty of Pacific College in 1928.

At the time of his appointment he had taught continuously at Pacific College from 1928 until 1941 except for two periods of war relief work and administration. In 1939 he was in the administration of food relief for all the southern section of loyalist Spain, a program in which approximately a million people were fed. In 1939-1940 he was in the administration of food relief for 6,000 Jewish refugees in Cuba.

Ironically, Gulley's close association with the American Friends Service Committee and its humanitarian stance to the neglect of more evangelical concerns of Oregon Yearly Meeting Friends served him well in administrative experience, but served him ill in a period of renewed evangelical concerns within the college constituency. Largely, but not wholly because of this, his tenure in the presidency became more and more tenuous until his final resignation effective in 1947.

Levi Pennington believed so strongly that Emmett Gulley was the right person to be president of Pacific College that the acceptance by the board of his final resignation led to one of Pennington's deepest hurts. If one were writing the history of the college from the vantage point of thirty years after the Gulley resignation and consequent termination, there is hardly any objective way to criticize the action other than on possible procedural grounds. But in examining the life and thoughts of Pennington it is necessary to unravel some of the threads of controversy and contradiction that reveal his perception of the incident. One can never be certain of having adequately separated the realities from the emotions in summarizing controversy, but something of the opposing perspectives can be clarified.

In his history of Oregon Yearly Meeting, *A Garden of the Lord*, Ralph Beebe points out in chapter VI, "Quaker Education in the Northwest," that during the 1920s and especially in the 1930s Oregon Yearly Meeting support of Pacific College gradually decreased, if judged by the number of Friends young people in the student body. During this era the Yearly Meeting was suffering from the polarizing effect of withdrawal from the Five Years Meeting. The more Bible-centered element which was instrumental in effecting the withdrawal was also becoming more dissatisfied with the administration of the college. The opposition by this group against Pennington during these years was building in strength as he experienced serious encounters with some of its more vocal leaders. Beebe states that following the Pennington retirement, leaders among the evangelical element spearheaded support for the college for about four years, but as it became evident that the new administration was following the same course as under the previous administration, dissatisfaction and opposition emerged with greater strength than before.

In short, there were two groups within the Yearly Meeting. For some time those considered more liberal continued to administer the college even after the evangelical group accomplished the withdrawal from the larger body of Friends. The next step within evangelical control was to give the college this evangelical quality, and in a real sense Gulley was too strongly identified with the humanitarian thrust of Quakerdom but too weakly identified with the evangelical stance to gain the confidence of evangelical leadership. Those who had actively opposed Pennington also opposed Gulley, and it seems only natural that the former president identified himself with the defenders of the new administration.

The emotional thrust of these controversial years emerged from the charges and countercharges of the two groups, both of which founded arguments partially on evidence, yet were dependent upon speculation. The college badly needed more students, it needed more gifts, it needed accreditation by the new regional accreditation association. It also badly needed both a stronger faculty and a more recognized educational program. Basically each group could claim that if its group controlled the college, these needs could be met, and there was some data to inspire belief in each claim.

Emmett Gulley first resigned the presidency immediately following the Yearly Meeting session of 1945, apparently the result of pressure from individuals who had attended the yearly session. Although his resignation was accepted, he was given a vote of confidence by the Trustees. This was the second paradoxical action within only a few days. The first had been commendation of the college for its "deep spiritual tone," given by the official visiting committee of the Yearly Meeting in its report,[15] and a like report from the Alumni Association. However, despite these words of approval they were followed by sufficient pressure from within the evangelical ranks to force Gulley to resign.

It is always difficult for any board charged with administering the affairs of an institution such as a college to evaluate internal pressures for change. In some measure this accounts for the wavering policy of support for Gulley by the Trustees. Following his first resignation he was given a five-year contract, which would lead an observer to believe this constituted an act of confidence. But in early autumn of 1946 dissatisfaction with his leadership began to mount once more, this time from within the faculty and students. At its October 28 Executive Board Meeting a student petition signed by twenty-five students demanded: (1) more frequent and more spiritual chapel services, (2) more effective leadership by the faculty and administration in the spiritual, social, and educational programs of the college, (3) an opportunity for students to meet with the Board of Trustees, and (4) more democracy in the operation of the institution.

In consequence, fifty-five students met with the Executive Board to present their claims in its November 8 meeting. After the students left the meeting, the discussion and charges became quite sharp, during which President Gulley resigned. His resignation was accepted. Among the claims made in the meeting was that more gifts could be obtained if the president were to resign and that a more qualified faculty could also be secured. Neither of these claims eventuated in reality, but within the next two months the records show that one substantial financial commitment and some smaller pledges were withdrawn, and the reason given by each donor was dissatisfaction with the termination of Gulley's presidency.

The significance of these events and situations for Pennington's life relates to three realities: (1) The financial condition of the college during the 1940s had been very strained, and since he had been influential in securing the gifts which Gulley had obtained, he knew that these sources would not support the college if Gulley were relieved from office. Levi saw the administrative change coming as a threat to the college financially, and at this time such a possibility could be a fatal blow. (2) He felt that the projected optimistic change in securing more competent faculty could not be accomplished simply by changing administration. Higher salaries was one of the first conditions for enlisting more faculty with doctorates, but almost of equal importance was the need for a more settled climate within the college. (3) Those who promised to bring about sudden improvements lacked the contacts and leadership necessary for accomplishing these goals.

Pennington's fears proved well-grounded for the immediate future of the college, because during the next decade and more the college suffered from a withdrawal of support by both groups. It was not until Milo Ross became president in 1954 that the evangelical support became significant.[16] Then began the slow healing of the deep wounds caused by the forced resignation of Emmett Gulley, and then a new recognition began to emerge for Levi Pennington's contribution and dedication to the college during the long, critical discouraging years from 1911 until 1941.

In attempting to present Levi Pennington's perspectives on the disagreements among Friends it is highly informative to read his own words. In late 1971 and on into 1972 Errol T. Elliott, Quaker biographer, wrote a number of letters to LTP asking him specific questions concerning his life and views. He was considering the possibility of developing a Pennington biography to include among the many studies of American Quakers as he had published in *Quakers on the American Frontier* (1969) and *Quaker Profiles* (1972). Among the many topics he asked Pennington to discuss was that of Quaker Controversies. His discussion, sent to Errol Elliott with a cover letter dated April 26, 1972, when he was only four months from his ninety-eighth birthday, follows:

> If we could select the wisest seven men and women in Quakerdom, and supply each of them with the seven secretaries that Herbert Hoover kept busy during much of the last ten years of his life, and if all that crew of more than half a hundred should work seven years on Quaker Controversies they could produce more than a five-foot shelf of books without solving one of the controversies.
>
> If I were asked for the one basic religious concept on which all Friends come nearest to agreement, I think I should say it is what I sometimes call the accessibility of God, the belief that the individual can reach God, can come into personal relation with him. But this one belief that should unite all Friends inevitably leads to endless differences and controversies. We can have an infallible Guide but because of our human differences and weaknesses we may not be infallibly guided.
>
> Few would question the proverbial wisdom, 'In essentials, unity; in non-essentials, liberty; in all things, charity.' But when it comes to the decision as to what are the essentials, there we run into irreconcilable differences, with me so righteously firm in my rightful convictions and the man who disagrees with me so jackassically stubborn in his wrong views that we just simply can't work together.
>
> And of course I'm uncompromising in my fidelity to truth. With many people, and with a large percentage of Friends which would not be many compared with the rest of the Christian world, compromise is a 'fightin' word, like liar, thief, traitor, and so on. I think of the incident in Tom Brown's School Days, when Tom and East and Arthur are discussing Naaman's proposed conduct with his kingly master in the house of Rimmon. Mention of the need for compromise sometimes, for which Tom said he was ready, and East remarked, 'Yes, Tom's ready for compromise. He only wants what is just and right; but when it comes to deciding what is just and right, it is everything that he wants and nothing that you want. Give me the Brown compromise when I'm on his side.'
>
> In a restaurant where I used to eat when I was a newspaper man and where transient travellers would sometimes try to cash bogus checks, and where no-good home folks sometimes try to have

meals charged for which they never expected to pay, there was a sign which read:

> We can't trust you for two reasons.
> First, we don't know you.
> Second, we do.

In the controversies that have annoyed us, that have troubled us, that have divided us into non-cooperating and sometimes hostile camps it can be said that some of them arose from the fact that we do not understand each other, and some from the fact that we do.[17]

Two addresses and one short article are included in this chapter for preserving three ideas he shared with others throughout the 1920s and 1930s.

Only the first of these is directly related to the agony theme of this chapter. Its significance is evident because it brings together almost his total reasoning for urging Oregon Yearly Meeting to remain in the Five Years Meeting. This is his position that must be allowed to stand in confrontation with the positions of those who favored the withdrawal, positions included within the text of the chapter. Inasmuch as the petitions and actions were included in their original form, Pennington's position must also be included without abridgment.

During the 1930s President Pennington gave a weekly radio talk over Radio Station KOAC, Portland. Frequently he was gone from Newberg, but when he was available, his was the voice speaking for Pacific College. In these talks he covered many topics related to Christian education, but his presentation, "Why Is a Small, Church-Related College?" seems especially significant to understanding his commitment to a small Christian campus, despite all of the detractions that could have destroyed a man with lesser vision and commitments.

The article which closes the chapter expresses Pennington's view of a Christian's attitude toward war. It is a good example also of his manner of taking issue with another who espouses a doctrine different from his, on what he considered a vital belief. Despite the hard stand he emphasized in this article, he was tolerant of those who did not share his conviction. This is documented in the manner in which he gave support to the young men in World War I who enlisted for combat service (Chapter II).

ON WITHDRAWING FROM THE FIVE YEARS MEETING
(May 2, 1926)

Friends will recognize that I am in an awkward position in speaking on this matter. I am a member of the committee of Oregon Yearly Meeting, the report of which as tentatively prepared is the matter at issue. To speak against the proposal to withdraw from the Five Years Meeting, which proposal is contained in the report of the committee of which I am a member, may seem an ungracious thing to do. But I am also Oregon Yearly Meeting's representative on the Executive Committee of the Five Years Meeting, and a member of some of the Five Years Meeting boards representing Oregon, and in view of these things I have had opportunities to know the Five Years Meeting from the inside which most Oregon Friends have not had. And I have some very definite convictions on the subject before us, and I am sure that no one thought nor would desire that my position on Oregon's committee should cause me to stifle my honest convictions.

I hope that nobody will think of this discussion as in any sense a debate between my good friend Carl Miller and me. We are simply asked to lead in this discussion, and however far apart we may be in some things, we are at one absolutely in our desire for the good of Oregon Yearly Meeting, the Society of Friends and the Kingdom of God.

May I just refer to his closing remark. He said that in his judgment some of our other Five Years Meeting leaders would have done better if they had resigned, as Ross Hadley did when the storm was raging about him. Well, I should feel, and I think some of our leaders would feel, that such a course would commend itself far more if someone could point out just what problems were solved, what criticism was stopped, what unity was secured by Ross Hadley's resignation. Personally I have said, not here but in their presence, that if I thought that the removal of any of our leaders would bring us to unity, though they were my blood brothers, I should favor such removal. No man's position or personal interest should be considered as above that of the church. I will go farther. If I were convinced that the break-up of Oregon Yearly Meeting would advance the interests of the Kingdom of God, I should favor it; if I felt that the disruption of the Five Years Meeting were for the best interests of the Kingdom of God, I should favor such disruption; if I believed it to be best for the Kingdom of God that the Friends Church should cease to exist— why, the interests of God's kingdom are paramount.

But to come to the real matter at issue. Oregon Yearly Meeting believes that the leadership of the Five Years Meeting is unsound, and therefore Oregon Yearly Meeting proposes to withdraw from the Five Years Meeting. I am opposed to such withdrawal for several reasons.

In the first place, if I may speak in medical terms, I do not agree with the diagnosis. I do not agree that the leadership of the Five Years Meeting is unsound.

Let us not forget that both the yearly meeting and the committee appointed by it have declined to make specific charges. It would seem that if our leaders are charged with unsoundness, they ought to have a right to face the charges, to know their nature, to know just what statements of theirs have led to these charges. Such information we have not given them, either as a yearly meeting nor as a committee of the yearly meeting, though a Five Years Meeting committee came for a conference with Oregon's committee, charged with the same investigation as to the loyalty of the Five Years Meeting leaders to the doctrinal pronouncements of the Five Years Meeting.

Let us not forget that various boards of the Five Years Meeting have issued pronouncements asserting their loyalty to the doctrinal standards which we have adopted; and especially has the Foreign Mission Board, about which so much criticism centers, taken definite action on our three-fold statement of faith.

Not only have our various boards taken such action, but the Executive Committee has done so, and if we are not familiar with their position, it is not their fault but ours.

And let me call your attention to this statement in a signed editorial of Walter C. Woodward, who is so much and so bitterly criticized. [Read from the editorial of March 27, 1924.] You see his attitude on some of these fundamental things, his attitude both officially and personally.

In view of all this and much more that might be given, I cannot feel that we are justified in declaring or believing that the leadership of the Five Years Meeting is doctrinally unsound.

But I object to Oregon's withdrawal for the reason that if the diagnosis were correct, the treatment prescribed would not cure the disease.

First of all, it would effect no cure in the Five Years Meeting itself. Suppose that there were unsound men in places of leadership in the Five Years Meeting. And suppose that therefore Oregon withdraws. Just what unsound leader would be reformed by that withdrawal? Or just what unsound leader would that withdrawal remove from office? Or just what leader of sound theology would our withdrawal from the Five Years Meeting put into a place of power in the organization which we had abandoned?

So far from curing any evils which might exist or which may exist in the Five Years Meeting, our withdrawal would put us beyond the power to help there. We should have no voice in Five Years Meeting counsels, no representation on her boards, no power in the national organization. We should have abandoned our right to protest—on what ground could we raise our voice against any evils which might arise in an organization which we had chosen to abandon?

I am opposed to Oregon's withdrawal because it would do us no good as a yearly meeting. We should have no greater liberty—who can name one point in which the Five Years Meeting has hampered us? We should have no greater unity—how could this be expected if part of the yearly meeting compels another part against its will to sever its connection with the great body of Friends in America? We shall have no greater power—if we have been wasting power in this controversy, we should waste it on this or some other if we withdraw from the Five Years Meeting. We would solve no difficulties by withdrawal. We have our differences in Oregon Yearly Meeting, and we should have them as truly if we were outside the national organization. I do not wish to say anything I should not about the work of Oregon's committee. But when in that committee meeting a statement was made as to the unity of Oregon Yearly Meeting, and I asked Clarkson Hinshaw as yearly meeting superintendent, if he could say what the other speaker had just said, it would have been interesting to you if you could have seen how eager some Friends were to participate in the discussion. It seemed that they did not want Clarkson Hinshaw to answer the question—and it was not answered. If we do not know that there are differences and heart-burnings right in the Evangelistic and Church Extension Board of our own yearly meeting, perhaps it will do us no harm to know it. We should not have our problems solved in Oregon by withdrawal from the Five Years Meeting. Some of them would be aggravated rather than cured.

And then I am opposed to this withdrawal because I believe that we should be starting something that we could not stop. We have been told that there are others in every yearly meeting who wish to withdraw from the Five Years Meeting. Well, the attitude of different Friends who favor withdrawal differs from those who take the position of my loved friend—and when I say loved friend don't you think I am joking for a minute—my loved friend Carl Miller, who holds that we need a central organization, but that in the interests of all concerned Oregon should withdraw from the Five Years Meeting, to the position of those who hold that "The Five Years Meeting is a thing which God hates." You read that, didn't you? If not, you've missed another opportunity. You know where that attitude centers, and of the advice that emanates from that quarter that we get out of this organization "which God hates," by yearly meetings if we can, if not by quarterly meetings, if not by quarterly meetings then by monthly meetings, and if not so, then man by man. With such an attitude and with others who for other reasons wish to break up our national organization, I fear that Oregon's withdrawal will start something that we cannot stop, and that may lead not only to the withdrawal of other yearly meetings but to a possible separation and schism in the church.

Again, I am opposed to the withdrawal of the yearly meeting because it seems to me there is a plan which is so much better from every angle. It was presented to the committee and did not win favor there, but I still think it is better than withdrawal. Let us remain in the Five Years Meeting, appointing our representatives, retaining our position of influence and power. Let us protest when things are in our judgment going wrong, retaining our position in the organization, so that our protest would have a weight which it could not have if we were no longer a part of the Five Years Meeting. Let us carry out, as a yearly meeting which is an integral part of the Five Years Meeting, the united program which is suggested by the report of the committee. If we cannot unite on such a program while we are part of the Five Years Meeting, what hope is there that we can do so if we withdraw? And having decided on the work in which we can unite as a yearly meeting with the rest of Quakerdom, let us try to force matters no further, but leave every meeting and every member free to cooperate with other yearly meetings in our united work still further, or to give no further cooperation, as seems right to the individual meeting or member. Surely there ought to be a way for us to retain our relationship with the other yearly meetings, which some of us prize so much, and at the same time preserve the unity of the yearly meeting.

There are so many advantages in united work that we ought to be willing to make sacrifices to preserve them. Aged ministers and missionaries, after serving Friends for years under such meager support that it is impossible to lay by anything, settle down to await death. Who shall care for them? The yearly meeting where they are living? The yearly meetings which they have served? They will not be cared for, in many cases, unless there is a central organization to look after the matter. Into every great city in America have gone enough Friends to make a strong Friends meeting, but in how few of them is there any Friends meeting at all. It is not the work of any one yearly meeting, but of all, and unless there is a central organization, the matter will not be attended to, and thousands of Friends will continue to be lost to our own denomination, which is bad enough, and to the work of the Kingdom of God, which is vastly worse. Pioneer fields by the score waiting for Friends, but the individual yearly meeting cannot care for them, and without a central organization they will not be opened. There is a great field for evangelism under the leadership of the central organization. You know that a former pastor of this meeting, a man for many years a minister of this yearly meeting, and for a number of years superintendent of the yearly meeting, is spreading the kingdom in a splendid evangelistic work under the Home Mission Board of the Five Years Meeting. Surely Friends who have been friends to the Indian and the Negro throughout our whole history should have a work among the Indians and among the Negroes—but we have seen much of it die because we would not support our central organization. Oregon Yearly Meeting could not handle the publishing interests of Friends, nor could any other yearly meeting; yet we need, we must have, Bible school helps, a national paper, etc. The peace work for which we have stood from the beginning—could Oregon handle that? Without a central organization America would be deprived of The Messenger of Peace, the one periodical which remained true to the Christian principles of peace through the Great War. And everybody knows the advantage of united work for that half of the world which has never yet had its chance for the gospel.

The Five Years Meeting is not perfect, Friends, and we all know it is not fully satisfactory. It is also true that Oregon Yearly Meeting is not perfect nor entirely satisfactory. Shall Oregon Yearly Meeting withdraw from the Five Years Meeting because it is dissatisfied with Five Years Meeting leadership? Then shall Newberg quarterly meeting withdraw from Oregon Yearly Meeting when it is dissatisfied with Oregon Yearly Meeting leadership? If not, why not?

Let us not withdraw, Friends. Let us stay in the Five Years Meeting, to exercise our power to restrain when she is going wrong, to guide in the right way, and to work with the other Orthodox Friends in America for the advancement of the Kingdom of God.

WHY IS A SMALL, CHURCH-RELATED COLLEGE?

(Pacific College Talk over Radio Station KOAC, Wednesday Evening, October 21, 1936.)

Good Evening, Friends.

I am glad to speak to you again, and in imagination to look into your faces, after a full year, so far as I am concerned, though I am sure Pacific College has been well represented during the twelve months since my voice was heard. In my mind's eye, while I look into this microphone, I can see friends of the college who in the past two weeks have written in about this broadcast, from Portland, Salem, Newberg, Corvallis, Scotts Mills, Bend, Springbrook, Rex, Glendale, and I do not know how many other places.

And on behalf of Pacific College I wish to extend sincere thanks to Radio Station KOAC for this privilege granted to the independent colleges of the state to speak to their radio audiences. I feel, and I suppose that most of those who hear me share that feeling, that it is a splendid thing to have this state-owned, noncommercial station, which can spread so much of genuine education, enlightenment and help to many who would otherwise not receive such help; a station whose maintenance does not depend on halitosis, nor b.o., nor any diseases of the digestive tract; a station which can go on with its work without the help of any form of liquor advertising and even without promoting the sale of any tobacco products. I am not intending any harsh criticism of radio stations which must maintain themselves by commercial contracts, though I wish some sorts of advertising could be kept off the air, which would be purer without them. But personally I am very glad for this state-owned, non-commercial station, and grateful for the privilege accorded the independent colleges of giving their programs over KOAC.

And now, even at the risk of seeming to repeat myself, I am going to attempt an answer to the question so often asked, "Why is the small, church-related college?" Of course the question does not usually come in exactly these words. Sometimes it takes this form. "We pay our taxes to maintain our state institutions of higher education. Why give additional money to maintain these private colleges?" Sometimes it takes this form: "Why do you people continue to work in a little church-related college, when you could make so much more money and have so much easier time working in big state institutions?" It seems to me that both forms of the question deserve an answer—and there are other things involved than any question of financial or other sacrifice, by faculty or friends of the college.

But first from the financial angle, the maintenance of the independent college is not an additional expense to the people of the state, but a genuine and a great economy. It is true that every independent college in the state is furnishing a college education for some students who would otherwise not be able to secure it, and is thus doing the state a real and great service. But most of the students now in the non-tax-supported colleges would, if these were discontinued, flock into the state-supported institutions, and the state would pay for their education in taxes, instead of having the independent colleges provide this education at no tax cost to the state. So that every man who gives to Pacific College to support its work, or to any other of the independent colleges, is keeping down the tax rate for state-supported education—very decidedly, for it will cost much more to educate a student in a state-supported institution than in Pacific College, for instance, largely because Pacific College teachers are doing their work at a great financial sacrifice because they do believe so thoroughly in the small, church-related college.

When I say these things, I hope I shall not be misunderstood as opposing state tax-supported education. We must have it, and it ought to be amply supported. Some of us would gladly see at least one addition to our present set-up, a thorough system of kindergarten education, with further improvements in public education, primary, grammar, secondary and higher education. But we believe thoroughly also in the place of the private church-related college; and for these, among other, reasons.

First, the small, church-related college can be selective. This does not mean necessarily that it will bar students with an I.Q. below the median—a state-controlled institution can do that. But it does mean that it can admit those who will work in harmony with its purposes and ideals, and decline to admit those who manifestly will not cooperate with those aims and ideals. With a relatively homogeneous group—even under these circumstances there will be plenty of clash and conflict to keep things alive— there is greater opportunity for advancement with less pull in the other direction, with consequent retardation.

In the second place, the small, church-related college can give an emphasis to certain aims and ideals which cannot well be given the same emphasis in the great state-supported institution. The great university can seek to advance character-development; but even in such matters some of us think the smaller institution has a decided advantage. "Character is more often caught than taught," and in the small college there is greater opportunity for the close contact of students and faculty which makes possible this much-to-be-desired contagion. The great university can seek to advance certain social and economic ideals; but with the mixed constituency supporting it by taxation, it is hard to avoid offending certain classes of citizens, whatever social and economic ground may be taken. And in the matter of religion the state-supported school has difficulty in advancing any definite religious ideals, with its constituency composed of Protestant and Catholic, Jew and Gentile, Mohammedan and Hindu, theist and atheist. The small, church-related college can, without offensive proselyting, uphold the religion of its founders.

Closely related to the faith professed by such an institution as Pacific College is the motive of service to humanity. "Not to be ministered unto, but to minister" might well be the motto of the follower of Christ as it was His. Surely the showing which the church-related college can make along this line ought to be truly impressive. In the last quarter of a century, for instance, almost exactly 75 percent of Pacific College's graduates have entered the "sacrificial callings." Nearly two-thirds have become teachers, some later to become housewives, some missionaries, some ministers, some Christian Association workers, some business-men, etc. One out of three has entered the definite service of the church in some capacity. One out of six has entered the whole-time service of the church in some of its denominations, as pastors, home and foreign missionaries, Y.M.C.A. and Y.W.C.A. workers, etc. And during and following the World War, in pro-portion to the size of its student body and alumni, Pacific College sent more of its young men and women into war relief service than any other college in the world.

In a narrower sphere the church-related college finds a reason for its existence, and that is in the service of the denomination with which it is connected. Less than half of Pacific College's students are members of Friends, the church to which the college is directly related; and not by any means all Pacific College graduates who go into the service of the Christian enterprise serve in the Friends church. But there are almost a score of Quaker preachers among our graduates, more than half as many Quaker college educators, and missionaries in Africa, China, India, South America, Palestine and other parts of the earth whose impetus to the service of the church came while they were students at Pacific College. In scores of church positions graduates of Pacific College are serving the Friends church, all the way from humble positions in the local church to the general secretary of the Five Years Meeting of Friends in America, the highest office among Friends in the United States.

But after all, it may be insisted by many that the small, church-related college must stand or fall on the basis of its purely educational achievement, on the intellectual basis, not the moral, the character, the religious, nor any other basis but that of intellec-tual advancement. Well even here the small, church-related col-lege does not have to be too modest. There is no man on earth who can lift as much at arm's length as I can lift right down at my side, and the teacher in the small college has his load very close to him. In a recent nation-wide achievement test at the close of the sophomore year, Pacific College's class stood in the third quarter of all colleges examined in the native intelligence of its sophomores—not surprising, since we are not as rigid as many colleges in enforcing intelligence tests on prospective entrants. But in the achievement test, our class of sophomores was not in the third quarter, but in the first. We had, if that test proved anything, got some real education across to that sophomore class, in the third quarter as to intelligence, but in the first as to achievement.

Well, my time is up, and I'm not nearly done. But perhaps you can see why I have spent more than twenty-five of the best years of my life in the office of president of Pacific College. And possibly I have given you a start at least toward the answer to that question, "Why is the small, church-related college?"

Good-night.

SHOULD A CHRISTIAN GO TO WAR?

(This article was originally written as a letter to the editor of *The Sunday School Times*, followed by its publication in *The American Friend*, April 9, 1942, pp. 159-160.)

The recent article by Dr. William L. Pettingill on, "Should a Christian go to War?" seems to me so full of error and so certain to mislead that I am venturing to offer a bit of a reply to it; not an exhaustive one, but one which touches just a few of the propositions brought out in this article.

It is true, as acknowledged by the author, that on either side of the question of a Christian's duty in war men [are] "equally godly, equally devout, equally sincere, equally brave." This truth is matched by the fact that in modern war there are men of this character among the citizens on both sides of the conflict. Is it the duty of English and American Christians to kill German and Italian Christians and the duty of German and Italian Christians to kill English and American Christians, and thus advance the cause of Christianity? Could anything be more unreasonable, or unchristian?

The attitude that it is the Christian's duty to obey the State, and that it might become his duty to perform an execution at the command of the State, seems to me so antagonistic to Christ's teaching and example that I wonder you could ever have permitted such teaching in your periodical. The State required the early Christians to worship the emperor or die. They defied the State, and died. Has the State a right to demand that I execute a criminal in violation of my conscience, and may it become my duty? I deny it absolutely. I should as soon admit that the state has the right to demand that I manage a state liquor store, or handle the gambling business of the State, or control licensed prostitution. There have been times, there is now such a time in many nations, and there will be other times, when the Christian must make his choice between the commands of the State and the commands of God. And the early apostles gave the rule for a situation of that sort that will never be abrogated: "We ought to obey God rather than men."

The basic tenet in this article, that God has set up two institutions in the world and ordained them on two different bases, the Church based on mercy and the State based on justice, seems to me utterly untenable. Unless there is a proper degree of mercy in the justice of the State, and a proper degree of justice in the mercy of the Church, both institutions, in my judgment, fall short of God's plan for them. God is both just and merciful.

The ideal that "the highest function of government is the judicial taking of life" is as repugnant to me as is the statement that "every government official is an 'ordained' minister of God." That would seem to mean every man in official position, no matter how he got there, nor for what purpose he won, stole or usurped his position. Hitler, Mussolini, Ivan the Terrible, the late Kaiser, Napoleon, the most corrupt practises in America—all these were or are government officials, "ordained ministers of God," according to this article. I cannot think that God recognizes them as such, even if Dr. Pettingill does.

For they are government officials, and surely the author of this article cannot be so naive as to suppose that only *our* government is ordained of God. We more than once resisted the English government; we warred against the Spanish government after they had granted every demand we made upon them; we fought the German government in one war with Italy on our side, and now we are fighting both of them, with England, our former enemy, on our side along with other powers which once were enemies. Is the present Russian government ordained of God? Was it a few short months ago when Russia and Germany were allies? This article seems to me hopeless in its efforts to justify a Christian's participation in war in obedience to his God-ordained government. The genuine Christian ought to know more about God's will for him than do these government officials, though every one of these, according to this article is an "ordained minister of God."

The appeal to the Old Testament for the justification of war seems to me puerile. One could quite as easily—to me it seems much more easily—justify slavery and polygamy and concubinage, the execution of a man for violation of the Sabbath, the killing of an entire family for the sin of one member of it, and many another custom which to me seems far below the level of the requirements of Christianity.

This article seems to ignore the fact, which to me the scriptures themselves clearly indicate, that God has given to man a progressive revelation. "God, having of old times spoken unto the fathers in the prophets, by divers portents and divers manners, hath at the end of these days spoken unto us in His Son." To me Christianity is far above Judaism. "Ye have heard that it hath been said" . . . "but I say unto you . . ." is a basic thing in Christianity. Christ completed what Moses could not complete. "An eye for an eye and a tooth for a tooth" . . . "resist not him that is evil . . ."—there is a real difference here. "Blessed shall he be that taketh and dasheth thy little ones against the stones" . . . "Father, forgive them; they know not what they do"—there is a real difference between the attitude of the baby-killer and that of the forgiving Christ.

To me the whole question resolves itself into this: Would Jesus go to war in obedience to the demands of his government if he were on earth today? Would Jesus stand behind a machine gun and mow down men and send them from the hate and blood-lust of battle to appear before the judgment seat of God? Would Jesus drop bombs on defenseless women and children? Would Jesus help to maintain a blockade that would starve human beings by the million? Would Jesus help, if he were here, to turn the land and the sea and the air into a hell on earth? These are some of the things that modern war means, together with wholesale moral and spiritual degradation for generations. For me it would be blasphemy to say that Christ would participate in carnal warfare; for me it would be heresy to say that he would require it of his followers. War is not the Christian way. There is a better way; and the sooner Christians find it and follow it, the sooner will come the day when "nation shall not lift up sword against nation, neither shall they learn war any more."

Notes to Chapter IV

1. *OYM Minutes*, 1918, p. 13.
2. *OYM Minutes*, 1918, p. 42.
3. *OYM Minutes*, 1918, p. 44.
4. *OYM Minutes*, 1945, p. 13.
5. Family Papers (FP).
6. *OYM Minutes*, 1919, pp. 32-34.
7. *Ibid.*
8. (FP).
9. *OYM Minutes*, 1919, p. 33.
10. *OYM Minutes*, 1920, p. 18.
11. *OYM Minutes*, 1924, p. 10.
12. *OYM Minutes*, 1924, p. 18.
13. Transcripts of the meetings held April 11, 25, and May 2 are in the Family Papers.
14. This address is included at the end of Chapter IV.
15. *OYM Minutes*, 1945, p. 40.
16. David Le Shana, who succeeded Milo Ross as president, has continued his close tie with evangelical leaders, and under his leadership George Fox College has made advances hardly dreamed of in the 1940s. Upon the foundation laid during the Pennington years, Oregon (Northwest) Yearly Meeting has built a college with an effective financial management resulting in an excellent physical plant, a strong faculty, and an enlarged enrollment.
17. Errol Elliot.

CHAPTER V | Recognition

> I came to Pacific College thirty years ago, having only three years
> of college attendance as an undergraduate, no graduate work, no
> experience as a college teacher, and no association with Pacific Col-
> lege before I was chosen as its president.[1]

THESE LINES form a part of the closing statement of Levi Pennington's final college report to Oregon Yearly Meeting in 1941.
This was a notable commencement season because of the special
programs and recognitions commemorating the half-century mark
of the college. For celebrating this occasion, the Board of
Managers authorized a history edited by Veldon J. Diment, *The
First Fifty Years.* Commemorative ceremonies began on Saturday
evening with a music recital given by members of the music faculty: Earl Wagner, Florence Tate Murdock, and Robert Hirtzel. For
the first time, the Baccalaureate Service was held on a Sunday
afternoon; in it President Pennington addressed the graduating
seniors and community. The special Fiftieth Anniversary program was held on Monday afternoon featuring a history of the college by Professor Amos C. Stanbrough of the first college graduating class. In the evening, a special recognition banquet was held
honoring President and Mrs. Pennington upon the completion of
thirty years of service to Pacific College. Significant within the
commencement program on Tuesday forenoon was the conferring
of the first honorary degree by the college, and appropriately it
was given to Herbert Hoover, ". . . its most distinguished son."
The Doctor of Humanitarian Service was, "In recognition of his

leadership in the relief of suffering in Belgium, Germany and other countries of Europe, his work for victims of floods and other disasters in America, his encouragement and direction of the movement for child welfare and other humanitarian causes, his present efforts to save starving people in Europe."

The banquet in honor of the Penningtons' years at Pacific College held a great deal of meaning to President Pennington. Appropriately, the theme of the program was "Service," and each of the seven speakers reviewed areas of his dedication and service. This was a word that appears to have best characterized his thirty years in Oregon, for the toastmaster was Dr. Burt Brown Barker, vice-president, University of Oregon, and recognition of his effective service was given by Dr. Edward L. Clark of the Independent Colleges of Oregon. Recognitions were also given by other members of the community and college which highlighted his distinctive personality as a teacher and administrator. Genevieve Cole gave the recognition presentation for the Alumni Association under the title, "Vivid Impressions." Although no copy of her presentation is extant, those "Vivid Impressions" remaining with her are both striking and informative:

> . . . we all called him 'Prexy' when we thought no dignitaries were around, though of course it was no secret. There must have been a reason—at least I know why I called him that. We realized, if dimly, that the college was his main interest—his hobby as well as his mission. His image was partly father, partly teacher, partly disciplinarian and partly entertainer, besides president. When basketball games were in full swing, he was ever present—yelling encouragement to his team. If he didn't like the referee's decisions, he let it be known with a roar. I remember seeing him walk right down on the floor protesting, wearing the old, grey felt hat with his grey, curly hair sticking out in the back. When we made any outstanding contribution—a prize, an honor, a success, a win or an academic achievement, we received a warm letter of commendation—always prized. We knew he would defend and support any effort for old gold and navy blue.

> Chapel, you remember, was daily and compulsory. The faculty sat in dignity on the platform and took turns providing the program. When it was Prexy's turn, we anticipated hopefully that he would announce another trip to his 'attic.' I was often moved and inspired by those writings, bringing us beauty, humor and

wholesome truths. I regret having missed his classes because he was away raising money when my turn came. He was sometimes gone most of a semester. I am sure there isn't an alum who doesn't appreciate the amount of time and effort he put into building our endowment.

I respected his masterly disciplining, having experienced it firsthand. I was called on the carpet for climbing in the dorm window after hours. I don't recall much that he said except that at the end he assured me I could be one of the finest Christian women in Oregon if I so chose. I remember leaving his office with a dim determination not to disappoint him. This was a 'line upon line' which spoke to that of God in me. I appreciate it.

His fund of funny stories was endless. I sat by him at the Junior-Senior Banquet when I was a Junior, feeling honored and a little apprehensive. He entertained all within hearing distance with one story after another and he completely fooled me with that one about the seven lean kine.

So the Prexy label was partly respect, partly friendship, partly pride in him and partly deep affection—our response to his particular personality and character. Prexy had his share of 'human nature' which we saw once in a while, but he had elements of greatness that have been a means of character building in my life. For all he meant to me as a student of Pacific College, I am deeply grateful.

The retirement dinner was only one of many special events held in his honor throughout his long life and career, but only a few of them will be highlighted to supplement those treated in earlier chapters. In addition to these special events, the full force and influence of Pennington's life and service can be appreciated best by noting the widely divergent quarters from which recognition came to him: honorary degrees, friendship with nationally known leaders in a variety of fields, speaking for important events, and continuous coverage by the press.

One of the first recognition dinners held in Pennington's honor as the President of Pacific College followed a communitywide drive for endowment, spearheaded by church and business leaders throughout the Portland community in 1920. This event celebrated what now might be regarded as a small accomplishment, but reaching the completion of a $25,000 fund drive in 1920 during the aftermath of World War I for a college which had held unpopular positions during the war amounted to a highly satisfying triumph.

He was honored on anniversary occasions many times, but the press coverage of his twenty-fifth anniversary as president was especially meaningful to him. This may have held special meaning because it provided a moment of calm in a time of storm as pressure mounted from some quarters of the Yearly Meeting. This recognition reinforced his conviction that he ought to remain with the college.

A bust was presented to the college in his honor, April 28, 1944. It was conceived by Dean Ellis F. Lawrence of the University of Oregon, and the sculpture by Professor Oliver L. Barrett also of the University of Oregon. The unveiling was by Barrett's widow Kathryn Barrett. Little remains by which to evaluate his response to this honor, but in light of his frequent reference of other occasions and the seldom-made reference to this one leads one to suspect that there is something about this kind of recognition that made response difficult for him. An altogether different feeling accompanied the hanging of his portrait by his daughter Mary Pearson when it was unveiled in the lobby of Pennington Hall.

Levi Pennington was especially moved by the decision of the Board of Trustees to name a dormitory in honor of him and Rebecca as is evident in his remarks made at the ground-breaking ceremony for Pennington Hall at George Fox College, May 6, 1961.[2]

The events through which Pennington was honored in the week of his ninetieth birthday, August 29, 1965, were especially meaningful to him. Recognition began a few days before his birthday when, in a Yearly Meeting session, he was called forward in the sanctuary to receive a tribute by the Yearly Meeting superintendent followed by the presentation of a great, oversized card. This gesture held much more significance within his recognitions than a casual recording of the event indicates, because it was an act of utter goodwill extended to one who had felt an alienation from some within this group for many years. In its truest sense this act undoubtedly opened a final decade of appreciation for him within the Yearly Meeting.

Levi T. Pennington in office at Pacific College.

*Levi and Rebecca Pennington in their home at
1000 Sheridan Street, Newberg, Oregon.*

*Fishing at home of Hollingsworth Wood
in Mt. Kisco, New York.*

*Levi and
Rebecca
Pennington.*

Levi T. Pennington and Herbert Hoover at Newberg, Oregon, on the occasion of Hoover's 78th birthday, August 10, 1952.

Levi T. Pennington, 91 years.

A few days later, the Newberg Rotary Club, to which he belonged for many years, declared a "Levi Pennington Day" in Newberg. The program of the luncheon consisted of nine speeches of recognition for his service to the community since 1911. Although the program was long, exceeding its normal time, he arose upon being made a life member of the club and gave a stirring impromptu speech of appreciation for the community that was strongly moving to a hushed audience of Rotary members and guests. On his birthday, August 29, the Alumni Association of the college held an open house in his honor in Pennington Hall to which some 250 guests from a wide geographical area came to greet him, in addition to a countless number of telegrams and letters sent by those who could not greet him in person. Seldom does a town the size of Newberg devote such an extended time of recognition that reaches all areas of its life to one of its own citizens who still is one of its residents.

Pennington was deeply moved on his ninety-eighth birthday when his family held a large open house for him at his granddaughter's home in Westtown, Pennsylvania, in order for many of his friends in the East to greet him. As on all of his birthdays when he was honored he said of this new age, "I became 98 years old for the first time."

Birthday celebrations held for him were more than simple recognitions that he had reached another mile marker in his life. This was one way of conveying appreciation for his long, active years of service to the church, to a community, and to a state. Thus there was no magic to the 29th day of August in the closing days of summer that gave one more number to Pennington's legendary chronology. The date presented another opportunity for his friends to congratulate him for the accomplishments of his life, many of which had gone unheralded through his active years before retirement.

Dr. Cecil Pearson said in an interview that among the recognitions of which his father-in-law, Levi Pennington, felt most proud were the academic degrees, both earned and honorary. He was proud that Earlham College had granted a Bachelor of Arts degree to him, already a man in his thirties. He wrote a long letter to his father in 1923 upon completing his Master of Arts degree in English at the University of Oregon. He felt that his final oral examination was exceedingly broad and difficult because it wandered far afield from British and American literature, and he was gratified to be granted the degree when it had been undertaken in such small periods of time at the university, sandwiched in between teaching, fund drives, and speaking engagements.

Early in 1923 President Leonard W. Riley of Linfield College asked Pennington for permission to present his name to the Linfield Board for approving an honorary degree for him. He answered President Riley that he was not sure if a Quaker ought to receive a Doctor of Divinity degree, but that he would give some thought to it if the Linfield Board could allow him some time before giving an unqualified approval; however, within his response of February 13, he included a resume' of his education, significant positions held, and related experience as requested.

What convinced him to accept the degree? All that is known for sure is that shortly after giving his consent, he wrote to Dr. Rufus Jones explaining why he had recently consulted a listing of several distinguished Quakers who had accepted such distinctions, and who listed the degrees after their names on important occasions. He then concluded that if other Friends were doing this he could see no reason for refusing such a title. Of course Dr. Jones was among those to whom Levi referred.

He appears to have been without any such reservations thirty-seven years later when Earlham College invited him to receive an honorary Doctor of Laws degree. In a letter from President Landrum B. Bolling of Earlham, February 19, 1960, Pennington was informed:

Dear Levi Pennington:

It is with great pleasure that I write to inform you that the Board of Trustees at its meeting on February 13 has voted unanimously on a recommendation that Earlham faculty confer upon you an honorary doctor's degree at commencement Sunday June 5.

We very greatly hope that it will be possible for you to attend this commencement program and to receive this well-deserved honor from your alma mater.

If there is any problem in the way of your coming, I hope that you will let us know. We want very much to try to arrange whatever is necessary to make sure that you are here for this occasion. I am sure that other members of your 50th anniversary class will be anxious to see you here in person. All good wishes,

Sincerely,

Landrum B. Bolling[3]

At the commencement exercises, Pennington's classmate Lilith Farlow presented him for the degree with the following citation:

> President Bolling, it is my happy privilege to present to you for the Honorary Degree of Doctor of Laws, Dr. Levi T. Pennington, a distinguished member of the Earlham class of 1910.
>
> On this fiftieth anniversary of his graduation from Earlham College it is fitting that this honor should come from his alma mater to a man who has devoted his life to Quaker education and who has made outstanding contributions as a religious leader.
>
> Levi Pennington was born in Amo, Indiana, in 1875. Even before he attended Earlham he had taught school, edited a newspaper, and served as a pastor in Michigan and Indiana. At Earlham he won prizes as an athlete, a student, and an orator.
>
> Immediately after graduation he was called to the presidency of Pacific College in Newberg, Oregon, where he served for thirty years. On leaves of absence he went on speaking tours throughout this country and the British Isles. He was ever active in the National Educational Association and other educational groups.
>
> Levi's fame as a speaker and a preacher has extended far beyond Friends and he has been in great demand among many groups for his unfailing wit and wisdom. He is also known for his writings on religious, educational, philosophical, and literary subjects.
>
> His classmates of the Class of 1910 united with the Earlham community and the larger community of Friends everywhere in rejoicing that this recognition is to be given to one who is universally beloved and esteemed.

This was a distinctive honor conferred by a college with a long tradition of excellence in education which could select a large number of graduates who had made national and international reputations in the fields of their endeavor. That Pennington was chosen for this honor testifies to the high regard with which he was held.

Although Pennington was well acquainted with nationally known Quaker leaders such as Rufus Jones, he was also a friend of other leaders in Christian circles. He had spoken in the same conferences as Dr. Daniel Poling, the longtime head of the Christian Endeavor Society, and he was known by such nationally known evangelists as Gypsy Smith. There is little need to document these associations, but some of his associations with other types of leaders may call for exploration. Probably no figure with whom he corresponded and occasionally visited and entertained held his admiration so strongly as President Herbert Hoover. Their correspondence began in 1925 and continued through the next forty years of Hoover's life. Except for considerations of relief and peace, and later in connection with the restoration of the Minthorn House in Newberg, Oregon, Hoover's boyhood home, most of their correspondence was social. It concerned greetings at Christmas, birthdays, special family events, and visits, rather than being substantive in the normal sense. However, it is this type of continuous letter exchange that shows the particular relationship they enjoyed.

Levi related his personal meeting with Hoover quite a number of times and all of the accounts agree in the principal details. In his essay, "More about Herbert Hoover," written following his address at the memorial service held for Hoover in Newberg (1964), he recalled their first meeting.

I was back in the eastern part of the United States to seek financial help for Pacific College, of which by this time I had been president for some years. Rufus Jones, knowing that I was to see Herbert Hoover, said to me, with a strange combination of Quakerly 'plain language' and unQuakerly slang, 'Don't let him get thy goat. He will sit there while thee talks, and so far as thee can tell, thee might as well be talking to a stump or stone; but he won't miss a thing.' This prediction proved to be entirely accurate.

My appointment to meet Mr. Hoover was late in the afternoon. It was at the height of the Teapot Dome scandal, and the Secretary of Commerce had just come from a long cabinet meeting. I was told, though he did not tell me, that he was fighting about the issue as to whether he should resign from the cabinet, one member of which had to serve a term in the Federal prison for his crime, and in the minds of many people the Administration was not clear of blame in the nation-shaking scandal, or whether he should remain in the cabinet and help clean up the whole mess.

He entered his private office where I was awaiting him, and I was shocked as I looked at his face. It was so drawn that it looked like the face of an athlete finishing a two-mile race in which he had put every ounce of possible energy into the finish and was ready to drop.

He gave me a word of greeting and we shook hands. Then I sat on one side of a great flat-topped desk and he sat at the other side, with nothing on the desk but a pencil and a letter-size scratch tablet. He picked up the pencil and while I talked he used the pencil on that tablet and never raised his eyes until I told my story.

Taking notes, was he? Certainly not. Near the center of that page he had drawn a little equilateral triangle. Then crossing this triangle he drew another, and he had a six-pointed star. . . . He never got that second doodle finished. I had finished what I had to say, and he had not missed a thing.[4]

Mr. Pennington had called upon Herbert Hoover for assistance in a financial campaign, and without particular commitment to influence some of his western business friends, their responses soon after his visit was indicative of Hoover's influence upon them.

The first visit of President and Mrs. Pennington with the Hoovers occurred also while the Penningtons were already in the East. The exchange of invitation and response is included because the notes convey insight into both Pennington and Hoover, the former with his wit even in a formal context, and the latter's great economy of words even from a secretary.[5]

THE WHITE HOUSE
Washington
November 24, 1930

My dear Mr. Pennington:

The President and Mrs. Hoover will be delighted if you and Mrs. Pennington will lunch with them at the White House at 1:15 Monday, December 15th. Please be good enough to advise me.

Sincerely yours,

George Akerson
Secretary to the President

304 Arch Street
Philadelphia, Pennsylvania
November 25, 1930

Mr. George Akerson
Secretary to the President
The White House
Washington, D.C.

Dear Mr. Akerson:

Mrs. Pennington and I are delighted to accept the invitation to lunch with President and Mrs. Hoover at the White House at 1:15 Monday, December 15.

If there is any special information which we should have as to just where, when and how to present ourselves, it will be appreciated. Naturally, our luncheons with Presidents of the United States have not been frequent.

With great appreciation I am sincerely yours,

Levi T. Pennington

THE WHITE HOUSE
Washington
November 28, 1930

My dear Mr. Pennington:

I have received your letter of November 25.

All that will be necessary for you and Mrs. Pennington to do will be to present yourselves at the front door of the White House a little before 1:15 p.m. on the day of the luncheon. The Chief Usher will be on the look out for you.

Sincerely yours,

George Akerson
Secretary to the President

Even though this was the first visit of the Penningtons with the Hoovers, it was not Hoover's first knowledge of President Pennington's effort on his behalf. Pennington had been an active campaigner for Hoover while he was seeking the Republican nomination, and again when he was running for the office. His speaking on behalf of Hoover was quite well known, and in some quarters there was a rumor that Pennington might make the nominating speech for Hoover at the National Convention. Whether this was more wishful thinking than a possibility is difficult to determine, but an article printed in *The Earlhamite* of Earlham College in March, 1928, is straightforward:

> It will be of great interest to Earlhamites to learn that Levi T. Pennington, president of Pacific College since 1911, is nominated, subject to popular election, for delegate-at-large to nominate Herbert Hoover at the National Convention to be held in Kansas City. Mr. Pennington is of the class of 1910.
>
> His fitness to make the presidential nomination speech is unquestioned. It will be remembered by some, and noted with interest by all, that Herbert Hoover attended the Friends Academy in that city where he lived with his uncle, before completing his college work at Stanford University. Walter C. Woodward, '99, remembers quite vividly a childhood debate against Hoover, who, however, was much older than he.
>
> In 1922 Herbert Hoover participated in the Diamond Jubilee at Earlham by making a public address before the audience assembled at the memorable occasion.
>
> Though a party prohibitionist, the Newberg Graphic urging Pennington to come out for the nomination, projected probabilities by adding that as far as the Republicans are concerned, no one could boast of a better representative. This seems especially interesting, since some will recall Hoover's hesitancy in declaring his colors before a previous presidential campaign.
>
> Results of the election will be anticipated since everyone admits L.T. Pennington's unusual qualifications for the position. Knowing Hoover's background as he does, he will be able to execute the mission more admirably and efficiently than one less favored. At present he is president of the 'Hoover-for-President Club.'[6]

The Friends generally took considerable pride in the fact that one of their own birthright members, from a small town in Iowa, later attending a Friends Academy in Oregon, had successfully gained the nation's highest elective office. Yet even they were not without their own kind of humor in anticipating his term of office. Following his election, Hoover went on a goodwill tour to South America leaving the press and other interested citizens to speculate on his cabinet appointments. During this information vacuum *The American Friend* decided to "scoop the news and honor contemporaries" by announcing, *"The American Friend* has undertaken the responsibility of selecting the new cabinet." Its appointments read:

Secretary of State . . . . Rufus Jones, Maine
Secretary of the Treasury . . . . J. Elwood Can, North Carolina
Secretary of War . . . . Levi Pennington, Oregon
Attorney General . . . . Carl Davis, Kansas
Secretary of the Navy . . . . . Frederick J. Libby, Washington, D.C.
Postmaster General . . . . Samuel Edgar Nicholson, New York
Secretary of the Interior . . . . . J. Passmore Elkinton, Pennsylvania
Secretary of Agriculture . . . . C. Claxton Terrell, Ohio
Secretary of Labor . . . . Alice Heald Mendenhall, Iowa
Secretary of Commerce . . . . E. Harrison Scott, Indiana[7]

There can be no doubt about the fun and sly irony involved in this article, but its purpose appears to have been one way of calling attention to the many able leaders within the Friends movement. The editors admitted to more than a slight difficulty in finding a suitable candidate for Secretary of War from among their leadership, but they finally decided upon Levi · Pennington because, they said, at the mere mention of war he was ready to fight.

Pennington received a number of letters from around the country following this article, congratulating him on his possible appointment. Many of these were quite serious letters, some from friends and others from those who only knew of him. The seriousness of these letters was puzzling until a number of clippings from scrapbooks began to reveal that some of the writers had not read *The American Friend* but only the story carried by newspapers. Even the *Newberg Graphic* treated the material quite seriously, so that it is little wonder that the press in Iowa and other places removed from Pennington's home territory caused their readers to think seriously of such an appointment for a strong Hoover supporter.

Following his term in office and his disappointing defeat for reelection Herbert Hoover devoted a considerable amount of time once again to the causes of food relief throughout the world. Within those efforts he became honorary chairman of the National Committee on Food for the Five Small Democracies. In that capacity he asked Pennington to serve on the committee for this organization, and upon receiving an affirmative reply wrote him:

December 13, 1940

Dr. Levi T. Pennington
President Pacific College
Newberg
Oregon

Dear President Pennington:

I was delighted to receive your acceptance of membership on the committee.

The whole committee deeply appreciates your support and I trust we may be of service in preventing a great tragedy. In any event we must make every effort and we must express American concern with their plight.

I enclose a statement which this committee has issued in respect to a recent statement reaffirming the British Government's policy.

Before I include your name on the list I would like you to know of it and consider whether you still feel that we should continue our efforts to find a solution for these helpless people. Please advise me of your wishes.

I am sending you the latest list of members, and we shall be issuing the further names shortly.

Faithfully yours,

Herbert Hoover

One recognition accorded Levi Pennington in association with Herbert Hoover which was very meaningful to him was the invitation to participate in the commencement ceremonies marking the fiftieth anniversary of Stanford University in which Hoover was given an honorary doctorate, in 1954. Mrs. Pennington was unable to accept Mr. Hoover's invitation to be their guest for the week preceding the ceremonies, so that Levi went alone. Dr. Pennington was asked to speak within the rather lengthy ceremonies, and his entire address bears evidence that he believed brevity to be the soul of wit. He said:

President Sterling told me that there was to be a great reform in the Stanford commencement. He said there would be no commencement address by some presumed great person. I presumed that he was relieving you of long boredom, and a long wait for that piece of paper that you have worked so hard to get. Then he promptly asked me to speak to you.

I gave fervent support to his reform on behalf of sixty-two generations of Stanford graduates who have suffered since I was in your spot. No doubt the long commencement address of my day was full of wisdom and advice but I do not recollect a word of it—I doubt if I recollected a word of it ten minutes after its delivery.

My mind was—like yours is right this minute—on something else. My total assets were this diploma and twenty dollars, twenty-two cents. My thinking was concentrated on what I was going to do next. Besides that, the night before our graduation, my classmates had met and repeated and most of us sang the father song of all blues. It was written by the class poet and entitled, "The Cold, Cold World."

Now in keeping with Dr. Sterling's reform, not to keep you waiting, I give you three short observations—but no advice.

Observation number one: You are stepping into your second great adventure in life—the first being when you came here. It will be a new adventure every day for the next sixty-two years.

Observation number two: You will not find this a cold, cold world. It is full of elders who wish our country to grow in grace and mind. They will gladly help you if you need it.

Observation number three: God bless you.[8]

Over the years there were a great many visits between Hoover and Pennington. Mr. Hoover, an avid fisherman, frequently sought the isolation of Oregon streams in the summer for trout fishing. When these brief trips took him to the northern part of the state he nearly always called on the Penningtons or asked Levi to meet him. After his retirement, the Penningtons spent a part of many summers with their older daughter Mary Pearson and her family in Greene, New York. In perhaps six of these summers, Pennington called on Mr. Hoover in his suite in the Waldorf Towers.

Because of this association, Hoover's letters to Pennington became more relaxed; frequently he signed his name Herbert H. But usually he maintained his sparse message with few words. One exception was a letter written to Pennington to express deep appreciation for what his experience at the academy had meant to him through the years.

The Waldorf Astoria
New York, New York
May 19, 1941

My dear Dr. Pennington:

I would indeed be glad if you would convey my greetings to
the faculty and students at Pacific College at this commencement
season. It is so long ago that I became a student at the then Pacific
Academy that I hesitate to mention it. But the recollection of it and
the ideas implanted by it are vivid and lasting. That is where I
gained a love for mathematics and science. It is where I had my
first glimpse of a great world of literature and languages. If I still
believe in the moral and spiritual foundations of civilization, that is
where it was implanted in my mind.

And Pacific College has done this service to thousands of other
boys and girls over these years. It has done it through the self-
denial of the students, of the faculty, and of the people of Newberg.
Is that not a service worthwhile for America?

Yours faithfully,
Herbert Hoover

During the 1950s much of Pennington's correspondence with
Hoover was related to the work of the Herbert Hoover Foundation
of Oregon, a group of concerned citizens who wished to preserve
Hoover's memory in Oregon by restoring his boyhood home in
Newberg. This nonprofit corporation was organized with its of-
ficers: President, Burt Brown Barker; Vice-President, Mrs.
George Gerlinger; Secretary, Hervey Hoskins; Treasurer, F.C.
Colcord; and directors, Levi T. Pennington, Emmett Gulley, and
Mrs. Laura Paulson. They secured the former home of Dr. Henry
John Minthorn, foster father of Herbert Hoover, and began its
authentic restoration of both exterior and interior furnishings,
with the cooperation of many interested organizations including:
the Oregon Society, Daughters of the American Revolution, Sons
of the American Revolution, National Society of Colonial Grand
Dames of America in the State of Oregon. The work was executed
by Miss Elizabeth Lord of Salem, assisted by Miss Edith Schryver.

Dedication of the memorial house was planned in conjunction
with the celebration of Hoover's eighty-first birthday, August 10,
1955. This was the largest occasion of the many in which the
citizens of Newberg and other citizens of Oregon joined together
to honor Mr. Hoover, and certainly one of the most enthusiastic

sponsors of the day was Pennington, despite his age. The private luncheon held in the dining commons of George Fox College preceding the public ceremonies was organized and conducted in a manner suitable for a former president of the United States, for which both he[9] and the president of the Foundation[10] expressed deep gratitude. This celebration was a significant day for the city of Newberg; it brought great satisfaction to Pennington personally because it honored one whose life had served those humanitarian concerns for which he too had given much time and energy over many years.

The fact that Herbert Hoover always remembered Levi Pennington on special days becomes a commentary on a relationship that if not always too personal, was nevertheless built upon mutual interest and admiration. This underlying understanding seems to come to the surface in the letter written by Hoover upon the death of Mrs. Pennington:

The Waldorf Astoria Towers
New York, New York
October 13, 1960

My dear Friend:

Words are wholly inadequate but I well know what you are experiencing and my deepest sympathy goes out to you.

Rebecca was a great lady.

Yours faithfully,

Herbert Hoover

Because Pennington had spent so many years researching the life of Herbert Hoover he became a kind of walking encyclopedia on the details of the Hoover family and its roots. For this reason he was among those asked to give oral interviews when data on the life of Hoover was being gathered from knowledgeable people for the Herbert Hoover Presidential Library, West Branch, Iowa, and the Hoover Institute on War, Revolution and Peace at Stanford University. His copyrighted interview with Raymond Henle, director of the project, has become part of the Hoover information.

Levi held many politicians in low regard because of their activities which are covered under the rubric of "political" or "practical." This was not the way he regarded those in elected office whom he observed living out their convictions, and for this reason he was always proud of a young Oregon citizen who was rising in national prominence during the late fifties and sixties. At the time of Hoover's eighty-first birthday celebration in Newberg, Mark O. Hatfield was still a professor of political science and dean of students at Willamette University in Salem while also serving in the State Legislature. He attended the luncheon and the public ceremonies with more than a nominal interest because he, like Pennington, was both an admirer and a student of Hoover's political philosophy. As a graduate student at Stanford University, Hatfield had written a thesis on Hoover, and if this was not sufficient for him to gain Pennington's respect, his concern for peace and his humanitarian ideals were. On the other hand Hatfield appears to have had an unusual respect for the ideals of the Newberg community and for George Fox College. His becoming one of its Board of Trustee members while still governor of the state bears further witness to this interest.

Hatfield highly respected Pennington because of his long contribution to Oregon, and he accepted Levi's words of caution and concern. It is natural then that as governor and then as Senator Hatfield he was careful to pay public respect to Mr. Pennington when he addressed any part of the Newberg community. Pennington wrote letters to newspapers, to state legislators, and to congressmen and senators in Washington, D.C., whenever he objected to the turn of events which he believed could be changed. He took special note of those who might be sympathetic to his interests and that included Senator Hatfield. One letter and response between them only five months before LTP's death seems indicative of their mutual understanding:[11]

November 25, 1974

Hon. Mark O. Hatfield
Senator from Oregon
Senate Office Building
Washington, D.C. 20002

Dear Friend: —

Every time I think of the thousands of illegitimate children left by our military personnel in various parts of Asia, I get all worked up and eager to do something besides giving my two-bit contribution through the Pearl S. Buck Foundation. I am in favor of aid to poor and needy whites, even though I know that in some cases they are to blame for their own poverty. I am in favor of help to needy blacks, though I cannot agree that the white race is responsible for this situation as much as the blacks believe. But there is no question who are responsible for these abandoned illegitimate children. It is our military representatives, our "brave soldier boys"; and while it is a national disgrace, I believe that the United States should assume responsibility for these helpless children, and provide for all of them till they reach the age and ability to be self-supporting.

Is Congress making any move in the direction of caring for these children? If not, why not? We are giving help in many places where we are not nearly as responsible and where the need is not so great.

With the hope that you have a happy Thanksgiving, and with best wishes always, always and all ways,

Sincerely your friend,

Levi T. Pennington

United States Senate
December 6, 1974

Mr. Levi T. Pennington
1000 Sheridan Street
Newberg, Oregon 97132

Dear Mr. Pennington:

Thank you for your recent letter regarding the United States aid to Vietnamese children of American personnel formerly stationed in Southeast Asia.

You will be interested to know that the Foreign Aid Bill recently passed by the Senate authorizes $10 million for child care programs in South Vietnam in fiscal year 1975. This is a $5 million increase in funds for that purpose from fiscal 1974.

One of the most tragic results from the Indochina war is the plight of millions of disadvantaged children left in its wake. The orphaned, the maimed, and the homeless are continuing victims of the violence in Indochina.

Again, thank you for taking time to write and share your thoughts with me on this matter of mutual concern.

Kindest regards.

Sincerely,

Mark O. Hatfield
United States Senator

Recognition by the news media does not always correctly project a human being's worth. At times such coverage represents only a fascination for the unusual, or the startling, or even the shocking. For the most part Levi Pennington enjoyed good relations with the newspapers of the Willamette Valley in Oregon, and their accounts of his activities were carried because his activities were interesting and had significance to the papers' readership. During the early years at Pacific College he was involved in fundraising campaigns, in accreditation efforts, in speaking at a variety of conferences and noteworthy events, most of which had press coverage. This gave him name familiarity in Oregon, resulting in more and more attention to his activities by the papers. Perhaps this accounts in some measure for the frequent news stories about him in his retired years. Although he lacked a public affairs agent to keep the papers informed about his coming and going, he wrote letters to the papers of his travel and speaking when out of state. Frequently these resulted in news stories about him.

He became a kind of authority figure for the press on anything touching on Quakerism; consequently, when special news stories broke on events such as the death of Herbert Hoover, he was interviewed by reporters who were writing in-depth, follow-up articles. At the time of President Richard Nixon's resignation the Portland *Oregonian* carried a picture of Levi in his rose garden together with an interview on his reactions to the Nixon presidency. When he was ninety-eight years old *The Oregon Journal* carried a picture of Pennington standing beside his newly acquired 1964 Chrysler, bearing the caption, "Not checked out yet at controls of 1964 Chrysler." The profile of Pennington's life was carried simply as a human interest story, centered in the fact that he was probably the oldest licensed driver in Oregon. This is the type of living legend that he became.

Newspaper stories on him were not limited to Oregon, because there was a continuing interest in his life in Indiana and

Michigan, where he had lived earlier and frequently visited. Only a few years before his death, the *Record-Eagle* of Traverse City, Michigan, carried his picture and a lengthy story of his life resulting from an interview by its reporter, W. Gardener Weber. This human interest feature grew out of Pennington's early association with both dailies, which eventually merged, the *Traverse City Daily Eagle,* and the *Grand Traverse Herald.*

Not all of the news stories centered in his life brought him comfort. There are times when the highlighting of an event bears upon its results in ways that are injurious. One glaring example of this was a story carried in the *Newberg Graphic* July 13, 1939, near the end of his tenure in the presidency. It has already been suggested that his closing years in office were filled with many tensions. He went before the board to argue that certain rules of conduct inflicted upon the students were now resented because of their unfairness. He contended that fewer and fewer Quaker young people were attending the college, resulting in more and more young people from other denominations whose expectations of their young people were quite different from that of Oregon Yearly Meeting. Because of this situation, he insisted, it was no longer right to impose rules upon them which they did not understand and that were not kept away from the campus. Pennington asked the board to relax some of these rules that were the most troublesome. The board took action to do so in its meeting May 12, 1939.

Soon after, the *Graphic* carried a front page story on this change under the headlines, "P.C. faculty no longer to be sleuths. Board gives students right to 'truck' off campus." The article then attempted to explain those actions falling under the "truck" designation as card playing, social dancing, and use of tobacco, as it explained, "The ancient laws of Pacific College putting an official ban on social dancing, card playing, and the use of tobacco slipped a notch last Friday when the college board held its quarterly meeting at Wood-Mar Hall." Undoubtedly many in the Newberg area felt that Pennington was a hero for advocating a change from what had been an unpopular stance of the college, but this misinterpreted the spirit of his recommendation to the board. He personally still believed in these standards, but he also saw them as being unfair to young people who wished to take advantage of the education given by the college, but who were denied this opportunity because of being forced to misrepresent themselves in order to enroll for classes.

The emphasis that has already been given to Levi Pennington's popularity as a speaker has suggested a great deal of recognition for this ability, yet it has tended to distort his image by being a diminution of his preaching. He was, perhaps, first a preacher in interest as well as in fact. Much of his recognition was from his special ability to communicate through preaching, resulting in his selection as a preacher for important occasions which called for special talents. The list of these occasions is too long to detail, but the invitation to participate in a memorial to distinctive Friends was meaningful to him and a few of these appearances should be mentioned.

On January 15, 1929, he preached the funeral sermon for one of his respected friends and fellow workers, Dr. Robert E. Pretlow. Dr. Pretlow was a dentist who felt called to enter the Friends ministry, which he served for many years as an effective leader. He began his ministry in Danville, Indiana, then after one year moved to Wilmington, Ohio, for the five years, 1901-1906. He then served a Friends Meeting in Brooklyn, New York, from 1906-1913, before moving to Memorial Church in Seattle for the next ten and one-half years. This was followed by full-time work with the American Friends Service Committee in war relief. For five years he was the presiding clerk of the Five Years Meeting, and in 1920 was their representative to the World Conference of Friends. Pennington's call to Seattle for preaching the sermon testifies to esteem for his preaching, as well as recognizing his association with Dr. Pretlow.

In April of 1942 Pennington was asked to give the memorial address for Dr. Walter C. Woodward in Newberg. Dr. Woodward had devoted a full life to prominent positions within American Friends, after growing up in Newberg, attending Pacific Academy with Herbert Hoover, and teaching at Pacific College. His father, Ezra Woodward, founded the *Newberg Graphic* and edited it for many years while serving on the Board of the college. Ezra Woodward's wife, Amanda Woodward, Walter's mother, has already been mentioned as the companion of Evangeline Martin who canvassed the community with horse and buggy raising funds for the administration building which bears their names, Wood-Mar Hall.

After completing his Doctor of Philosophy degree at the University of California, Walter Woodward taught history and political science at Earlham College. He became director of the Indiana Historical Society, chairman of the Board of Earlham College, and spent his last years as editor of *The American Friend*. He was widely known as a brilliant writer.

The issue of *The American Friend* of May 7, 1942, was in memory of Dr. Woodward with articles in tribute to his service to the church and its concerns. Dr. Pennington's stature is revealed by noting that his memorial address, "Dedication to Service," preached in Newberg was the fourth memorial included in the special issue, following that of Rufus Jones, C.E. Pickett, and R. Furness Trueblood.

Although not classified as a sermon, the decision for Dr. Pennington to give the inauguration address of Dr. Gervas Carey as president of Pacific College, December 12, 1947, was filled with significance. Gervas Carey followed Emmett Gulley as president in a critical period of both Yearly Meeting and college history, as has been discussed. Yet his address was directed toward bridging the gulf that had separated the two elements of the Yearly Meeting and college. He asked for loyalty for his long-time friend Dr. Carey who was coming to the college after many years of effective college teaching in addition to successful pastoral leadership. It is impossible to convey to anyone unacquainted with the situation how much this invitation pointed toward honoring a man who had given such long service to the college, but yet who also felt alienated from it during his early retirement years.[12]

A final sermon not referred to elsewhere held special significance to him, for he gave the address for the Herbert Hoover memorial service held in Newberg October 22, 1964, at the same hour of the memorial service held in the East.[13]

ON THE OCCASION OF THE GROUND BREAKING CEREMONY FOR PENNINGTON HALL GEORGE FOX COLLEGE MAY 6, 1961

First let me say that I deeply and sincerely appreciate the honor conferred on me and the wife who is gone by the name that this future dormitory is to bear. She deserved it for the many years of unselfish devotion and unstinted labor that she gave to the college, I cannot say untiring, for sometimes she was tired to the very heart of her. If I could speak for her as well as for myself, I would say a hearty thanks for both of us, as I do say it for myself.

There is always a temptation to reminisce at a time like this, especially to one who has lived forty years as often as I have, and I could not think of this occasion without remembering another in which I was concerned. It was at the time of my retirement from the presidency of the college. At the farewell meeting for me it was announced that I was not to speak, and the applause was deafening.

As I think of those who will spend their student days in this house-that-is-to-be, I know that they will be facing problems, but they can be sure that former generations have had their problems, too, not about piffling little things like trips to the moon, but about the newly discovered extra-galactic universes, millions of light years away, and moving away from our galactic universe at a speed of 160,000 miles a minute—or was it a second? How glad we were that they were not nearer, and not coming our way!

I hope there may be many thousands of man-hours and woman-hours of sleep in this building, rather than in the classrooms. But there will be times when sleep will not be easy; when problems physical, mental, moral, financial, social, spiritual, will keep students sitting at the desk and into one form of darkness or another, seeking light on some problem on which eternal destiny may depend. It is my hope that these students may find the wisdom that is beyond biology and mathematics and philosophy and theology, and may find that place of security by faith so that they can say with confidence as they retire for sleep,

And so in this vast universe of multiplied infinities
I trust in love as infinite as God, the great Creator,
And kneel, as in my childhood, and begin my prayer, "Our
　　Father."

And so I turn this first sod for the building that is to be, with the hope that all goes well with it and with all who dwell in it for all the years that are to be.

ADDRESS AT THE INAUGURATION OF
DR. GERVAS A. CAREY
AS PRESIDENT OF PACIFIC COLLEGE,
DECEMBER 12, 1947

Mr. Chairman, President Carey, Members of the Board, the Faculty and the Student Body and Friends of Pacific College:

The man in whose honor we have met today has undertaken a very difficult task, the presidency of a small, church-related college, an institution which has as its reason for existence the combination of definite Christianity with cultural education so as to produce and develop genuine Christian character.

Such a task is always and everywhere a difficult one. So great an advantage inheres in the situation of the tax-supported institution in all matters of finance and physical equipment that any institution dependent on other sources of income is under a serious handicap from the start.

And the college which emphasizes personal religion subjects itself to an additional handicap in the estimation of very many people. There are myriads who desire the advantages of the best in intellectual training and physical development, but who do not wish the demands which Christianity makes to interfere with any life plans which they may make.

And in addition to the difficulties which any genuinely Christian college must confront, Pacific College faces difficulties which many another church-related college escapes.

First, its denominational constituency is pitifully small and scattered, from the standpoint of what is generally recognized as a minimum for the successful operation of a church-related college. A membership of 30,000, not widely scattered geographically, is supposed to be the irreducible minimum, with 40,000 much nearer the norm. We have one tenth the latter figure, scattered over three great states.

Many a college was given its initial impetus by some lover of education who was able to make a large contribution in a financial way as well as by the earnestness of his desire to promote the advancement that college provides. Pacific College had no such inception. . . . The fathers and mothers of Pacific College were poor in all but faith and works. No millionaire philanthropist gave Pacific College a rich initial endowment. For twenty years after its foundation as a college, and more than a quarter of a century after the beginning of Friends Pacific Academy, out of which the college grew, its endowment was less than nothing. And after more than half a century of effort, the full cost of which is known to God alone, the endowment of the college is far from adequate.

Under such circumstances as these, with other difficulties which could be mentioned, Dr. Carey has taken up the task of presiding over the destinies of the college. What are the conditions under which, with the blessing of God, he has his best if not his only prospect of success?

First, he will need the earnest and whole-hearted loyalty and cooperation of those who *are* the college. It is easy to think of the present campus and buildings, the present board and faculty and student body as constituting the college; but such a view is too short-sighted. One needs to include the yearly meeting, one of whose enterprises is the college; one needs to include the alumni, as much a part of the college as I was a part of my father's family after I had left the old home and started life for myself; and surely one needs to include those members of former faculties who have given the best part of their lives to the service of the college. If President Carey can have the loyal cooperation of all these elements, he will have the largest human factor required for the success of all administration.

It is likely that not another man in the world could have been found who could come as near to commanding this loyal support and cooperation. He has the confidence of the yearly meeting, whose members believe in his integrity and Christian character; he has the confidence of the board, whose members believe in his quality as a scholar, his ability as an administrator, his soundness as a theologian; there is no known reason why he should not continue to have the complete respect and cooperation of the faculty and student body. Many of the alumni and former faculty members have not had the opportunity that those already mentioned have had to know him—the full confidence of these in part he has yet to win.

But these are not enough. Oregon Yearly Meeting, if all its aspirants for higher education should attend Pacific College, and that will never be, is not large enough to provide the student body that the college should have. Its influence should reach far beyond our denominational borders. "None of us liveth to himself, and no man dieth to himself," and the same is true of the individual church, of the denomination, and of the college itself. It would not be enough nor nearly enough if Pacific College could supply higher education to all the young people of Oregon Yearly Meeting. The college must reach out, not merely to educate and bring into our denominational fellowship those who are not now Friends, though that will inevitably result, but it must, if it is to fulfill its destiny, reach out in helpfulness to those of other denominations and to those with no church connection who need the help that a Christian college can give. It should serve its immediate community—there should be a steady stream of Newberg High School graduates entering Pacific College; it should serve its state—more and more should graduates of Pacific College be occupying positions of importance in its educational system, its government, its professions, its material and spiritual advancement; it should more and more serve its country, and the world, even though it is mathematically unlikely that it will ever again provide a president for the United States and the greatest server of human life since the world began. Thus to reach out to the help of those beyond our ranks will not require any abatement of our religious interest, though it will require tact and consideration for the feelings and attitudes of others. The same Bible which says "be holy" also says "be courteous."

And as Oregon Yearly Meeting is not a sufficient field for the college, it is not rich enough in this world's goods to finance the college properly, certainly not if other enterprises of the yearly meeting are to be properly financed. Without the assistance of members of Friends in other Quaker areas and of other friends of the college not Quakers the institution would long ago have gone to join the hundreds of other colleges that have failed to survive, not because they lacked high aspirations and noble purposes but because they could not command sufficient financial resources. The hundreds of thousands of dollars contributed by those who were not in any way constituents of Pacific College have made possible what it is today and what it is to be in the future.

And what is that future to be? Probably not one of us doubts that God has a plan for Pacific College, always has had, will continue to have.

We cannot dissociate ourselves from the past if we would. And what one of us can look with too much pride on the past?

There is perhaps no need to dwell on the past except in our secret souls to learn from it. Who is there who, if he could clearly see God's perfect plan, would not have to say, "We are unprofitable servants"?

And surely we should face the future with proper humility. There will need to be, on the part of all who have the welfare of the college really at heart, a deep and earnest seeking to know what is God's will. It is disastrously easy to seek to have God on our side; it is inescapably necessary to put ourselves on God's side.

If I should express a wish for the college of the future, it might well be a wish that it might fulfill that which stood for as many decades as its declared aim and purpose, expressed every year in its annual catalogue:

> Pacific College seeks to be definitely and positively Christian. It seeks to bring its students to an acceptance of Jesus Christ as personal Savior and Lord. It seeks to help its students to a definite dedication of life to the service of Christ, and to that incoming of the divine Spirit without whose help the fullest service to God and humanity is impossible. It seeks to assist its students to find their work in life, and at least to begin their definite preparation for it. It emphasizes constantly the ideal of service rather than selfishness, and of character as well as scholarship.

"Christianity and Culture" has been the motto on the seal of the college from its beginning. To that double aim is the institution dedicated. For the achievement of that aim, those who love Pacific College, and who love God are glad to commit the college to the leadership of you, Gervas A. Carey, Bachelor of Arts, Master of Arts, Bachelor of Divinity, Doctor of Divinity; and may God bless you and the college.

INTRODUCTORY ADDRESS FOR THE DEBATE ON UNIVERSAL MILITARY TRAINING

(Covered by Radio Station KEX, Portland, Oregon, Tuesday evening, December 16, 1947)

This proposal that peace-loving America should adopt universal military training, a form of peace-time conscription, is a revolutionary and hitherto un-American proposal. It is a part of a move in the direction of making America a military totalitarian state. More and more the military is extending its influence over our state department, our foreign policy, our schools, our government. We are now spending more *per day* on our military forces than the entire world is spending *per year* on the United Nations. And the proposed measure would make our present expenditure look like pocket money.

The burden of proof for such a revolutionary measure, as such men as Chancellor Hutchins, Senator Morse and many military men agree, is definitely on the proponents of the measure. And we are not dealing with minor details, which may be greatly changed as time passes, but with the main issue. One does not have to eat all of a rotten egg to know that it is rotten.

My position is that which is the regular position for the negative, to say of the arguments of the affirmative, in the language of the boy, first, "'Tain't so," and "What if it is?" We all want world peace and prosperity. The background of the affirmative argument is that there is no way to insure these desirable ends except to be prepared, by universal military training, to do more destruction of life and property than anybody else can. My contention is that such preparation for destruction is not the way to peace and prosperity but to war and bankruptcy; and that even if it is impossible to have peace and we must have war, universal military training is not the answer, but the training of a much smaller force of volunteer specialists in modern warfare.

Practically all church, educational, labor and farm organization is against this movement. It will cost from three to five billion dollars, in addition to our regular military expenditures. With millions of innocent people starving and freezing in the world, such a waste of money is inexcusable.

HERBERT HOOVER, THE MAN

(Address at the memorial service for Herbert Hoover at the Friends Church at Newberg, Oregon, at 9:30 a.m., October 22, 1964)

It is not easy to speak briefly of the character of a man whose personality was so many-sided that he could accomplish all the wonderful things of which we have been so forcibly reminded by the previous speaker. Volumes could be written about his versatility that gave him top rank as a mining engineer—he was named engineer of the century by the first engineering society in America: a commanding and increasingly important place in the business world—he gave up the certain prospect of great wealth that he might render great service to humanity; a great leader in government—his enemies thwarted much of his effectiveness and his friends were not wise enough to realize what he did accomplish till the passage of the years had cleared their vision; an author who wrote many of the things that the world needed to have on record, a record that no other man on earth could have provided; and above all, the indispensable leader in the greatest life-saving enterprises that the world has ever known, from the dawn of creation until today.

But I am to speak of his individual qualities, not his versatility. And first among these I should place his absolute, unchangeable, unassailable moral integrity. His enemies could attack his philosophy, his economic tenets; they could blame him for a world crisis for which he had no responsibility and which he could in large part have averted with the right political cooperation, but there was no flaw in his armor of moral rectitude. In his personal conduct, in his family life, in his business transactions, in his international affairs, in his handling of all the billions of relief from America to the ends of the earth, he maintained the high moral ideals that had been taught him by his village blacksmith father and his Quaker teacher-preacher mother, and later by his uncle and aunt with whom he lived during his boyhood and youth in Newberg and in Salem, and by the teachers in Friends Pacific Academy, where he was a student at its very beginning and where, according to his own testimony, he received the training that led him decades later to his vast fields of altruistic service. The Decalogue was vital law to him, as was its summary by the greatest of all his teachers, "Thou shalt love the Lord thy God with all thy heart—thou shalt love thy neighbor as thyself."

The second element of his character that I would have us consider has to do with the second great commandment which the Great Teacher declared to be like the first. Herbert Hoover loved his fellowmen. The black aborigines in Australia, the impoverished coolies in China, the terrified and starving men and women and children in Belgium, the Germans whom we had been taught to hate until many blind one-hundred-percent Americans considered it a patriotic duty to kick a dachshund simply because he was a German dog, the 20 million starving Russians in that most terrible of all modern famines which most folks did not know about and most of those who did have forgotten, for all these and many others, in our own land and in scores of other countries, the heart of Herbert Hoover went out in a way that took him and his queenly wife to the ends of the earth. Herbert Hoover loved humanity, and invested his life in helping men and women and children. His hand-written letters to children who have written to him, a few of which are printed in his book, ON GROWING UP, his leadership in Boys Clubs of America, and other things that seem so small in comparison with his leadership in the work for tens of millions, are simply other evidences of his love for humanity.

Another quality that contributed to his greatness was his invincible courage. Without it much of his work could never have been done. It was not merely the way he handled his tasks as a mining engineer, sharing in the perils of the men who worked under him and accomplished things that other leaders had declared impossible; it was not merely the heroism that he showed and which his devoted wife shared during the Boxer Rebellion in China; it was not merely his courage in crossing the North Sea again and again and again, not knowing at what second a German-planted mine or a German submarine might send them into eternity and carry out the German ideal of marine warfare in those days, "Sunk without a trace." He faced human perils greater than merely the perils of the material world. He was the man who could stand face to face with the German Kaiser and bring him to a decision which the imperious Wilhelm had scorned even to consider; he was the man who could oppose the Big Four at the council chamber who were seeking to starve Germany into the acceptance of a treaty that declared that the entire guilt of World War I was theirs, and to assume reparations that everybody knew they never could pay. Indomitable courage was one of the outstanding characteristics of Herbert Hoover.

Another outstanding characteristic was a remarkable combination of originality and independence. When he faced a problem, whether one of material nature or one in the more difficult area of human nature, he was likely to come up with a solution that nobody else had thought of, or that somebody may have thought of but had abandoned as impossible. This sort of situation arose more than once in his mining engineering work in Australia, where a new method accomplished the supposedly impossible. And while he was American Food Administrator, much of his work was accomplished by methods that experts were sure could not succeed. There was inescapable need for vast additional stores of food for American soldiers overseas and for others of the Allies, both in the field and in areas remote from actual combat; and the number of men removed from productive labor on the farms greatly increased the need for greater emphasis on increased production of food in America and decreased consumption of basic foods. Many in high places in government were sure that voluminous laws must be enacted to control the consumption of meats, sugar, flour and other eatables; and there must be stringent laws limiting gasoline consumption, with heavy penalties for violation of these and a myriad other laws that were considered necessary. Herbert Hoover believed that American citizens would cooperate when the need for cooperation in such matters was made clear to them. And as Food Administrator he carried out his ideals with a minimum of laws and legal penalties. And so we took our supposed quota of meat and shortening; we used jelly on our bread instead of butter; we ate potato bread and bean bread and corn bread and buckwheat bread, with never a taste of white wheat bread; we used our small quota of gasoline, and met all the limitations that "directives" put upon us—and were much the better as a result of our deprivations. Here, as in other activities, Herbert Hoover chose to be *the* Food Administrator. He knew what had to be done and he knew how to do it, and he did not want to be handicapped by others who knew so many things that weren't so.

Independent as he was, Herbert Hoover was loyal to the American ideal of obedience to law. He obeyed the law, whether he was fishing for redsides on the McKenzie or entertaining royalty in the White House. America was under national prohibition during his administration, and the executive mansion had the unusual experience of not having a drop of intoxicating beverage alcohol inside its walls, for society leaders from America or for royal potentates from overseas. The first time I ever met him personally was when the Teapot Dome scandal was at its height. He had just come from a cabinet meeting. One of the president's cabinet members was involved in violation of the law that landed him in a federal penitentiary, and the Secretary of Commerce, Herbert Hoover, was fighting out the personal question as to whether he should resign from a cabinet where such a scandal could center, or remain in the cabinet and help to clean up the foul situation. I never saw a face so drawn as his was except the face of an athlete finishing a two-mile race in which he had given everything he had. Violation of the law, in high places or in low, found no favor in the heart nor in the mind of the little Quaker boy from West Branch and Newberg—and presently from London, Berlin, Paris, St. Petersburg, Rome, Peking, Adelaide, Washington, Palo Alto, New York—and where not?

Another quality that endeared him to those who had the privilege of being his personal friends was his really delightful sense of humor. During much of his life there was little opportunity for him to give evidence of this quality. Too many people were dependent on him for him to have time to laugh—often he had no chance even to smile. He was not like Abraham Lincoln in this regard, much as he resembled Honest Abe in other particulars. Lincoln could throw off temporarily the great burden that was crushing the life out of him, and by some rollicking story that would convulse his auditors, with him joining in the laughter, he could ease the pressure of his terrible responsibility for a time, at least. But there was seldom such hilarity for Herbert Hoover. Day and night for many long periods he had to know that the lives of thousands, sometimes millions of men, women and children hung upon his ability to reach a right decision. But sometimes in private conversation among his chosen friends, with his wife, who was so definitely a complement to him, so definitely what he was not in some social lines, he could unbend, and laugh and joke and enjoy himself and add to the joy of others. And there came a time when, if he chose, he could delight an audience with his wit and humor. I was in one big gathering where he mixed humor with his very serious address, and got more than one hearty laugh, and I was in another great gathering in which his speech was interrupted again and again by uproarious laughter that fairly shook the house.

It would be hard for some people to believe that a man of such colossal achievements as those of Herbert Hoover could be genuinely humble, but he was. He did not consent to the restoration of his birthplace until after the death of his wife. When he finally consented to the restoration of the house in Newberg, where he had lived as a boy with his uncle and aunt, Dr. and Mrs. H.J. Minthorn, it was not to be the Hoover House, though most people call it that; it was to be the Minthorn House, as it is, officially. On one of his visits to Newberg I took him over to the college and showed him the simple plaque on the wall in Wood-Mar Hall which mentions briefly the steps from boyhood to world prominence, and his only comment as he turned away was, "Too flattering."

Indefatigable energy was another of Herbert Hoover's qualities. Work eight hours a day, ten hours, twelve, sixteen—sometimes twenty-four. Shortly before his 86th birthday a visitor was waiting till Hoover could see him, and one of the secretaries told the visitor that her employer was working from eight to twelve hours every day. "How can he do that?" said the visitor. "He is almost 86 years old." "Yes," replied the secretary, "but he doesn't know that."

When Lou Henry Hoover died, fate had come near to breaking the heart of this giant among men. Dr. Burt Brown Barker, who is president of the Herbert Hoover Foundation which restored the Minthorn House, and who was a boyhood friend of the former president and his friend until his death, said to me after Mrs. Hoover's death, "Herbert Hoover is the lonesomest man in the United States." But grievously as he missed the heroic companion of his heroic years, he threw himself into the tasks that nobody else could do, such as the writing of AN AMERICAN EPIC, and keeping as many as eight secretaries busy he completed this and other monumental works before age curtailed and at last put an end to his labors.

Herbert Hoover was elected to the presidency of the United States by the greatest majority ever given to a presidential candidate. He was defeated four years later by the greatest majority for his opponent in our history. The story of how the loved and honored world hero was brought down so low in the minds of his countrymen is one that is not appropriate to deal with here. The lies that were broadcast, the political opposition to every proposal for relief from the world depression that was a delayed detonation from World War I, (the president had just said to the Congress the day my wife and I were the guests of him and Mrs. Hoover, "You must not play politics with human misery" but they did)—the story of that "smear" campaign is not one of the most pleasing stories in American history. Many things about it are very hard to believe; but the most remarkable thing about it is the fact that Herbert Hoover never became bitter. Many of his friends were bitter beyond measure. Many of them still are, in spite of the efforts of some who participated in that "smear" campaign to make an atonement by writing about their victim some of the finest things that have been written about him; and notwithstanding the statement of Eleanor Roosevelt that Hoover was not responsible for the depression that contributed to his downfall. But Herbert Hoover maintained his equanimity; went about the work that was his, unembittered, and ready for any service that he could render to his country and the world.

And there came opportunity for great service, which he gladly rendered. America came to honor him again, as in the days before his election to the presidency. He came to be recognized as an elder statesman. The change had come rapidly, as had come the loss of favor with the people. At one national convention of his party the meager applause when he appeared was little less than insult to one who had held the highest office in the greatest nation in the world; four years later the spontaneous and long-continued ovation that was given him was like nothing else which that convention produced.

Now he is gone, and in every continent there is mourning for his passing. The son of the village blacksmith and the humble Quaker teacher-preacher, by what he was and by what he did became president of the United States and the world hero of the twentieth century. There is a passage in the Bible which says, "There were giants in the earth in those days." There are giants in the earth in these days, too, and one of them as a boy went to school here, fished in our streams, played with his schoolmates, did chores in what is now the city park named in his honor. We can think of him as the giant of vast world affairs, and we can think of him, too, as the boy, full of fun but full of earnestness. Of him as of Lincoln whom Lowell was describing in his Commemoration Ode, it can be said,

Here was a type of the true elder race,
And one of Plutarch's men talked with us face to face.

Notes to Chapter V

1. *OYM Minutes*, 1941, p. 50.
2. Text of this address is located among the addresses at the end of Chapter V.
3. University of Oregon Collection (UOC).
4. Text of this address is located among the addresses at the end of Chapter V.
5. The Hoover correspondence is from the University of Oregon Collection.
6. Shambaugh Library (SL).
7. From the Woodward Scrapbooks, Shambaugh Library.
8. (UOC).
9. Herbert Hoover wrote a warm letter of appreciation to Lydia A. McNichols, who directed the luncheon and served as its hostess.
10. Following is the note from Dr. Barker:
    To Mrs. Lydia McNichols
    With sincere appreciation for preparing the guest luncheon for Mr. Herbert Hoover on his 81st birthday, Aug. 10, 1955, in Newberg, Oregon, and for organizing the groups of ladies to assist you in this service. It was a complete success in every way. For this I wish to give you the warmest thanks of the Foundation.

    Burt Brown Barker, President
    The Herbert Hoover Foundation

    Newberg, Oregon
    Aug. 10, 1955
11. From the Hatfield correspondence, University of Oregon Collection.
12. Text of this address is located among the addresses at the end of Chapter V.
13. Text of this address is located among the addresses at the end of Chapter V.

CHAPTER
VI

Benediction
1948-1975

LONELY

Since you have gone away
    I am alone, dear, and sad without you.
Since you have gone away
    Earth seems bitter and dead to me.
Though you have gone away
    Memory longingly lingers about you
I am so lonely, so lonely, dear,
    Since you have gone away.

THIS EIGHT-LINE LYRIC written after the loss of his beloved Rebecca in 1960 expresses an ever-present loneliness during the last decade and a half of Levi Pennington's life. He suffered an emptiness following his retirement of which he often spoke to his family and celebrated in poetry, yet his behavior revealed little of his inner distress. Instead of withdrawing in his retired years, he continued participating in the causes and crusades with which he had long been identified. He worked actively with the American Friends Service Committee, with relief programs following the Viet Nam and Korean military actions, and continued his dedication to saving civilization from the scourge of war and its aftermath of famine, disease, unwanted children, and homeless refugees. World War II found him as hardheaded an advocate for peace as he had been in World War I, thus in addresses such as, "What is America's Road to Peace" and "The Path to Peace," he continued to explore alternatives to war. One week after Pearl Harbor he challenged the Newberg Friends Meeting by his sermon,

157

"What Can the Christian Pacifist Do Now?" Following the war he participated in debates both by radio and before live audiences urging a rejection of universal military training.

During an interview, Errol Elliott remarked that Levi Pennington remained a conservative religionist all of his life, and one cannot examine his sermons, his prayers, and his letters without awareness of his strict adherence to those doctrinal positions held by evangelical Friends. He embraced these from his early years as a worker in Traverse City, into his years as a pastor among Indiana Friends, during his years as an educator, and into retirement. Many of his sermons sought to clarify Quaker positions: "Practical Modern Mysticism," prepared for the West Coast Theological Conference belongs in this category, and its closing statement admonishes:

> If to all our other approaches to God, intellectual, ritualistic, or whatnot, we add this mystical, supersensible, extra-intellectual approach, we shall find a wisdom which transcends all knowledge and a power which goes beyond all merely human energy. If then we follow the guidance of this super-intellectual wisdom, and labor in the commonplace tasks which must always occupy most of our time, in accordance with the nature of God of all Goodness who has deigned to impart Himself to us in mystical union, we shall be embodying in our own lives and service Practical Modern Mysticism.[1]

His use of the Bible throughout his sermons was that of one who accepted its authority as a "divinely authorized record of the doctrines which Christians are bound to accept," and for this reason he quoted from it continuously in supporting his positions. His Christology becomes apparent in his sermon, "What Think Ye of Christ?" preached to the congregation and radio audience of the Glenns Falls Meeting (New York). In it he declared:

> . . . Jesus Christ said with every confidence, 'All power is given unto me, in heaven and on earth.' And there is nothing in His life to throw a shadow of doubt upon His statement. At His touch the leper was healed, a blind man saw, the deaf heard; at His word the tempest was stilled, the demon was exorcised, the dead came back to life; under His smile of forgiveness the greatest miracle was performed, the miracle that showed His power both on earth and in heaven, for the libertines heard and the harlot's heart was cleansed and they were enabled to 'go their way and sin no more.'

Another statement of His that seems to be the limit of what He might have claimed was this, 'I am the way, the truth, and the life. No man cometh unto the Father but by me.'[2]

In another popular sermon he spoke on "The Fatherhood of God and the Brotherhood of Man" by emphasizing the fatherhood of God as the loving, the just, and the forgiving Father of mankind, a first step in recognizing the brotherhood of man. This sermon closed with two paragraphs unmistakably a declaration of the "Good News" which stands central to the meaning of evangelical:

> Every son of man is in a sense a son of God, and owes Him filial allegiance. Every son of man may be in a fuller and better sense a son of God by being born of God. When in this sense he has become a son of God, he owes to his Father and will faithfully render to Him his deepest gratitude, his fullest allegiance, his best service.
>
> And if he is truly a son of God in this fullest sense of partaking of the divine nature, he will share God's love for the world, even the unthankful and the unlovely. And with a warmth of genuine affection he will love his fellow-Christian, his blood brother in the household of faith—with a love that will overlook faults, minimize non-essential differences and show to the world real proof of discipleship. 'By this shall all men know that ye are my disciples, if ye have love one for another.'[3]

Pennington's general religious position is made clear in a Quaker message given at Western Yearly Meeting of Friends, "Eighth Month 18, 1968," entitled "The Double Duty of Friends for Such a Time as This." Within the introduction he sought to clarify his perception of the principle duty of the Christian Church of whatever denomination. Then he showed its relationship to the particular concerns of Friends. Throughout his life, as in this sermon, his highest priority was given to what he identified as the "Claims of the Gospel," but he expended a great amount of time and energy advancing and interpreting the particular mission which he understood as claiming the special attention of Friends. This address served both functions, and in it he said of the church generally:

> Now the thing that I am talking about is one of these—in a sense—subsidiary things to the main job of the Christian Church.

The fundamental job of the church of Jesus Christ in the world—Quaker or Methodist or Baptist, or Presbyterian or whatever—is to bring men and women and children into harmony with God, into relationship with God, into union with God by faith in Jesus Christ; and to train and help prepare them for the life that now is and for that which is to come. This is the basic task of the Christian Church, and can be done by no other agency. It is about some of these tasks that I am to talk this afternoon; and my effort in this lecture is to call to our attention some of the tasks that are peculiarly ours as Friends.

Pennington then outlined what he considered as the first duty of Friends:

And we who call ourselves Friends should feel a particular requirement to carry out this first responsibility in personal religious experience. We do not put our faith in outward form and ceremony. We do not expect our children to enter the Kingdom of God through infant baptism, nor later as a result of a confirmation ceremony. We do not trust in water, by sprinkling, pouring or immersion, to wash away our sins. We do not expect that literal bread and wine will bring us per se into communion with God. Everything we omit of the ordinances that other Christians find 'a means of grace' behooves us to have in reality what these ordinances stand for in the minds and hearts of other Christians.[4]

His address was given during the undeclared war of Viet Nam when America was engaged in probably its most unpopular war. For him the present emergency provided a renewed opportunity for Friends to propose a form of international relations that could preserve human life, not destroy it. He also raised the historical question of Quakers concerning the responsibility of responding to governmental calls for service which violated conscience.

It was Levi Pennington's conviction that Christians and particularly Friends should engage fully in bringing relief to those unfortunate men, women, and children who suffered from the effects of war. Motivated by this belief, he gave his full assistance to relief agencies, and moral support to his students who left college to administer food and clothing relief in Europe following World War I. In June 1919, as chairman of the Yearly Meeting Service Committee, Pennington reported that although five of their young men had returned home, twenty were still working in France and in other needy areas of Europe in soup kitchens for children, milk stations, child welfare centers, and food services for families. As his address was being given to Western Yearly Meeting in 1968 he was still active in the Heifer Program for Overseas Relief. He had served as its vice-chairman for the Oregon Committee during the previous year and was still on the Executive Committee. Many times he had written to his family of the weariness he felt in traveling throughout Oregon buying heifers. At times it was difficult to fill out car loads because of insufficient numbers of calves, but now in his nineties he continued his humanitarian efforts.

During the last decade of his life Levi thought about other things than the church, for it is obvious that he gave some attention to the way he might be remembered. There can be little doubt but that he gave some thought to the possibility of someone undertaking his biography. Although he disclaimed any such idea, the possibility rose to the surface in several scattered letters. When he was approached directly by Errol Elliott, he answered in a letter from Detroit on July 7, 1970, "The first thing naturally is the question as to why you or anybody else would want to write a biography of me." Then after admitting that if it were to be done, certainly, "I know of no body who could do it better than you . . . nor do I know of any-body that I would rather have do it."

He gave one stipulation that ". . . this biography, if it ever comes into existence, will bear a date after the one that will be on the other half of the memorial stone that bears the name of Rebecca." He was anxious that if a biography were written that it not reflect unkindly upon those who had opposed him openly. He apparently envisioned a recounting of his life that would explore the events of his life more than his thoughts.

In agreeing to donate the majority of his papers to the University of Oregon, he requested that they remain sealed until after the death of four men whom he named, or until after his own death, a precaution that seems unnecessary now since the actions and events which caused his major estrangement are matters of official record. It is to be assumed that he was concerned about some of his irate letters; however, if this were his thinking, he need not have worried because only a few of these escaped the flames of his fireplace.

His reluctance to give approval for a biography was probably a mixed reaction, in part it was real, in part modesty; it may have been giving an expected response, or it may have been tongue-in-cheek. However, he left behind the materials for which a biographer dreams. The large quantity of material poses some problems because it is impossible to know how carefully it was selected. If the destroyed material blotted out one side of his personality, then that which remains is not representative; however, this is almost certainly not the situation. That he burned many files of correspondence purposefully seems clear from his own statements, but the gaps now remaining do not appear to result from a systematic purging. Some of these gaps can be filled in part from the quantities of correspondence which were not in his house at the time of his destroying effort. Enough of the problem remains that one researching Pennington's life from his papers must frequently draw the line between what for him was trivia and what was significant. Even when this arbitrary selection is done by observing some ground rules, it still does not preclude the possibility of emphasizing the wrong thing, to the neglect of something he might have wanted emphasized. Of course there is the necessity for reassessing his life now in the light of different values than he would have recognized. Each generation writes its own biography of past leaders because a life takes on new significance with each change in interest. A many-faceted life thus becomes a new subject; because the previously neglected contribution now becomes the thing of interest, it takes on a new relevance.

Pennington might have been shocked if he had thought his ideas were recognized as significant to the history of Pacific College and to Friends. His actions appear to have loomed large in his thinking, but to a generation interested in motivation, in analysis, and in evaluation, that which lies behind the actions themselves becomes a viable subject of investigation and report. Thus he could not have anticipated any more than others in the past what to destroy and what to keep, in order to preserve a particular image for a biographer.

Levi Pennington's strong faith in God, his concern for the world, his complete good will, his convictions, and his interests can hardly be identified more clearly than in his public prayers. His graceful use of language, its simplicity and straightforwardness as he addressed the one from whom he came, and to whom he would some day render an account of his life, conveys his most unconscious expressions of faith. Two prayers given at the Friends United Meeting are illustrative:[5]

Prayer July 20, 1966

O Lord our God,

We recall the record of long ago, in simpler days than these, with much fewer men and women living on the earth, that 'The Lord God came down to see the city' that the world that Thou has made and that man by his sin has so sadly marred; Thou seest so many millions war-mad, hate-crazed, blood-drunk; so many blind and deaf to the best things of life; and we, looking with our imperfect sight must harden our hearts or break them.

We would gladly change the world if we could; but we look at ourselves and realize how impossible the task is, few and weak and lacking in wisdom and power we are, and we are in despair—except as we look to Thee for help. Thou has laid help on One who is mighty. Help us to link ourselves with Him, that the impossible may become possible, the dream and the hope for better things become reality as we belt ourselves to the drive wheel of the universe, as we make available through our humble selves the power that is back of the atomic power of the Almighty to bear our problems . . . . Right in each humble station represented here may we bring the power of the Almighty to bear on our problems, that Thy Kingdom may come and Thy will be done, in us, among us, and through us to the ends of the earth.

In the name of Jesus Christ, our Saviour and our Lord,

Amen

Prayer July 23, 1969

O God, our Gracious and loving Father,

Thou who holdest the extra-galactic universes in the hollow of Thy hand and who answerest the prayer of the little child, with gratitude for the blessings of these days and all the days of our lives, we ask Thee that more and more as the days pass we may realize our ideal and Thine that we should be indeed a united meeting.

United in one faith, faith that Thou art neither dead nor dying; faith that Thou has not abdicated Thy throne nor turned the control of all that is over to another; faith that Thou art as accessible to us as Thou wast to Moses or Isaiah or Paul or Martin Luther or George Fox or any other heroes of Thy Kingdom; faith in the saveability of the human race: united in our hope—hope for the better days based not only on Thy promises but also on what Thou has done in other days darker and more discouraging than these: united in our love, our love for Thee, the supreme goodness; our love for our brothers, white or black or yellow or red or brown; our love for those on the other side of the earth and meeting that other requirement that is sometimes harder, love for our brother who disagrees with us; united in our determination to know and do Thy will, confiding in that promise given to us through Thy Son, 'If any man willeth to God's will, he will know.'

Thus committed to Thy will and to our task, may we serve Thee and our fellowmen faithfully and acceptably.

We ask in Jesus' name.

Even in the last decade of his life Pennington did not withdraw into a mystical, contemplative retreat from the world. He still walked to the platform of the Newberg Friends Church and sat with the ministers each Sunday morning. He walked more and more slowly, and his great frame was less erect each year, but his participation in the service remained decisive and strong; his pleasant, modulated voice still hushed the worshipers as he prayed, or testified, or spoke of a concern. He frequently gave the benediction, through which his Christian outlook and faith become clear.

The themes running through these benedictions form a commentary on his most serious thoughts, interests, and concerns during the last three years of his life. He approached the benediction of the morning worship service as a solemn moment of worship in which he spoke his deepest concern to God in faith. Through them a reader can trace the calendar as he prayed for a new year, then gave thanks for the hope springing from the Easter experience. As the year moved on he gave thanks for the birth of our nation and he prayed for those in leadership. His thoughts then moved toward the Advent, and finally he reflected on a closing year.

A frequent theme was that of man robbing God. He asked for faith "to ask," for a sense of mission, for courage to accept the will of God, and for the dedication to make the most of the present. At times he expressed anxiety for the now, a reemphasis of a continuing theme. In many addresses he had said in effect, "Now is the only time we have." Two additional themes deserve attention: advancing the kingdom of God, and unity. The former he phrased in different ways but he conveyed this deep urge through his variety of image: often it was being businesslike with God, or performing our function in the body of Christ. But his utter good-will to those about him is given special recognition in his prayers for unity, unity of spirit, unity with those about him, and unity in loyalty to Christ.

Although he frequently mentioned in letters and in public that he might not be present at the end of another year, he seldom touched upon that subject in his benedictions. However, as can be noticed in his benediction of December 9, 1973, his prayer carried the theme of being ready to meet God.

BENEDICTIONS[6]

December 24, 1972

Our hearts rejoice our Father,

As we remember again that Thou didst so love the world that Thou gavest Thine only begotten Son that we through faith in Him might live. Help us each one to realize that the birth of Jesus, the life of Jesus, the death of Jesus, His resurrection, His ascension, His coming return to earth, are for us—for men—for everyone of us—however unworthy we may be. For us, the Word became flesh and dwelt among us. And we pray Thee that in our hearts may be fulfilled the prophecy, "He shall see the travail of his soul and shall be satisfied." Be born in us O Christ, that we may suitably repre-sent Thee to a world whose supreme need today, as every day, is harmony with God through Jesus Christ our Lord and Saviour. Help us that we may keep Christ in Christmas by keeping Him in our own hearts.

In His own name we ask it,

Amen

December 31, 1972

Our Gracious Father,

We are gathered here under such happy circumstances with so manifest blessings from Thee surrounding us while other millions are suffering. Help us to be grateful for our situation with the blessings that have been ours during the past year however little we have deserved it. And help us as we look forward to the coming year to realize that if a year from today or a year from this Sabbath day there should be a meeting of worship here, that some of us will not be here. Help every one of us to say in his heart right now "I may be one of those who will not be here a year from now." And with that consciousness may we face the coming year to be ready at any time because we are faithfully following Thee. Help us to realize that we do have an infallible guide. And help us also to realize that though we have this infallible guide, we may not be infallibly led unless we follow close so that we can hear His voice so that we can be directed day by day. With this responsibility upon us may we face the future recognizing with Thy servant of old that our times are in Thy hands. Do be with us we pray Thee God. Do guide us we pray Thee Holy Spirit. We thank Thee for Thy great love to us O Christ. Help us not to hold back anything from Thee.

We ask it in Jesus' Name,

Amen

February 4, 1973

At home I have a piece of paper little more than half the size of this sheet (4x6). Its worth, I suppose, about one-tenth of a cent as paper but it has my name on it and it has the name of a sum of money on it and it has a signature on it. Now I can take it to the bank tomorrow and I can get that sum of money because of that signature. The man who signed that has money in the bank. Jesus said to His disciples, "Hitherto you have asked nothing in *my name*, now ask in my name."

Lord, teach us to pray in the name of our Lord and Saviour Jesus Christ,

Amen

February 18, 1973

Our Father in heaven,

We thank Thee for Thy great love that sent Thy Son as heaven's great missionary to the earth. We thank Thee for Paul, perhaps the greatest missionary after Jesus Christ, who said, "I am debtor both to the Jew and to the Gentile, both to the learned and to the unlearned." We thank Thee that the God of love wishes to supply every need of humanity according to His riches in glory by Christ Jesus. Bless especially we pray Thee, those who go from our greatly blessed civilization to others whose need is so great as was the need of our ancestors when they were the toughest race of savages in Europe. Give wisdom, we pray Thee, to those who go as Thy representatives to those of other races, other colors, other civilizations, that they may have wisdom to know how to present the claims of Jesus Christ in the most effective way. And above all, give to us who do not go but who send, the sense of mission, the sense that we are truly debtors as those who devotedly go to other countries and give their lives there. Help us that our lives will be given here and that we may seek always to pay our debts, recognizing that we are indeed indebted to all the world. Dismiss us with Thy blessing, go Thou with us we pray Thee, may we serve Thee acceptably every day.

For Jesus' sake,

Amen

March 11, 1973

We would pray with Thy servant of old, "so teach us to number our days that we may apply our hearts unto wisdom." And help us to remember that we never go over this part of our lives again and to make the most of today and every day for ourselves and for those who are called to minister in the home, wherever we are and in Thy service O God.

We ask in the name of Jesus Christ our Lord and Savior,

Amen

March 18, 1973

Our Father,

We pray Thee that we who have named Thy name may exercise the faith that worketh by love. Give us a faith beyond acceptance of any system of words, a faith that ties us up to the power of God through Jesus Christ our Lord. Give us we pray Thee the faith that worketh by love that we may be true followers of Thy Son Jesus Christ who went about doing good and who said to His followers, "as the Father hath sent me, even so send I you." Go with us we pray Thee, as we go to our homes, give us, oh give us the faith that ties us up to the power of God in this world and the next.

In Jesus' name we ask it,

Amen

March 25, 1973

Our Father in heaven,

Help us to seek earnestly to love God as we ought to, to serve Him through service to mankind whom we are to love as we love Him. Dismiss us with Thy blessing and benediction we pray thee in Jesus' name,

Amen

April 8, 1973

Our Father in heaven,

We are grateful to Thee that Thou has made it possible for us so to believe in Jesus Christ and so to accept the will of God for us that all shall be well for us today and all the days that are to be. Help us we pray Thee, that we may face the future in loyalty, complete loyalty to Jesus Christ and His teaching, that all may be well with us.

In Jesus' name we ask,

Amen

April 22, 1973

O God our Father,

We thank Thee for the privilege of knowing and worshiping the supreme hero of all ages—Thy only begotten Son who defeated Satan in the wilderness, sin on the cross, and death in the tomb. We thank Thee for the supreme hero and victor and that Jesus Christ is alive today that we can follow Him. That since He rose we may walk in newness of life, seeking those things which are above. May we walk with Him here that we may be with Him in eternity.

In His name we ask it,

Amen

May 6, 1973

Our Father,

Help us to remember that our greatest achievements, whatever else we do and accomplish, are the things which we accomplish in the spiritual world. And help us to realize that whether we are trying to influence others, we are doing it anyhow by what we do, and by what we say, and by what we think, and especially by what we are. Help us to love Thee supremely, help us to love our fellowmen as we ought that we may advance Thy Kingdom by our influence in every way.

In Jesus' name,

Amen

December 9, 1973

Our Father in heaven,

We remember the words of Thy Son speaking of the end of things. Then as Thy final word was, "Be ye also ready," that should be (we are sure) the concern of every heart here. Whether the end should come to an individual (anyone of us here) in an auto accident today, in a heart attack, or a stroke or should come after long suffering, or whether we should live to see that day when Christ comes, with the voice of an Archangel and with the trump of God, when every eye shall see Him, even those that pierced Him, help us to be ready, as Jesus enjoined us.

In His name we ask,

Amen

December 30, 1973

(After singing a song without accompaniment, Dr. Pennington then spoke the following benediction.)

Dismiss us with Thy blessing, we pray Thee. And go with us all the days that may be. May we follow Thee, keeping the spirit of Christmas and of Calvary in our hearts and exemplified in our lives.

For Jesus' sake,

Amen

January 6, 1974

Our Father in heaven,

We pray Thee that Thou wilt help us to be as businesslike with Thee as we are with the government and the grocer. Help us to know how much we ought to turn back of the gifts that Thou hast given us to the direct work of the church and how much more of the tithe we can give. Help us to remember that we are told that God loves an hilarious giver. Help us to be joyful in our giving to the limit of our ability. May our devotion to the cause of Christ be complete, financially, as in every other way.

For Jesus' sake,

Amen

July 28, 1974

Our gracious Father,

We pray Thee that this service may not have been in vain. Wherever Thou has spoken to any heart here—in song or in testimony, in sermon or in the quietness of our heart before Thee, whatever Thy word has been to each one of us, may we obey the voice of God now and always.

In Jesus' name,

Amen

July 7, 1974

Our Heavenly Father,

We pray Thee that every soul who has named Thy name may say to himself now, "there is a place for me in the service of God and man in this church," and help us find our place. We remember the words of the poet who said, "Life may be given in many ways and loyalty to truth be sealed as bravely in the closet as the field—as bravely in the kitchen as in the pulpit." Help us to serve Thee and to remember the actual fighting in a war is done by a buck private in the rear ranks quite as definitely as the commander-in-chief. Bless these men who have been called to leadership, bless us that we may not fail them as they may not fail us, and that none of us may fail Thee.

For Jesus' sake,

Amen

August 4, 1974

Our Father,

We remember that the prophet speaking for God reprimanded Israel because they were robbing God of tithes and offerings. Help us to remember that the tithe is not the upper limit of our giving but that God expects offerings from us, He that gave the best that heaven had for the worst that the earth had produced. Help us to be true to Thee not only by giving what Thou hast given to us in things but because Thou hast given us hearts that love Thee and that love mankind. May we give ourselves and all we have to Thee.

For Jesus' sake,

Amen

August 17, 1974

We thank Thee our Father,

That we have an all-sufficient God, and through Jesus Christ we have access to omnipotence, omniscience of God. Help us to believe that in all our ignorance, Thou knowest and art willing to show us enough of Thy wisdom so that we can follow Thee and do our duty. We thank Thee that wherever we may be Thou art there. We thank Thee that all the power is committed into the Son through whom we have access to all the power we need to do all the service that Thou requirest. Help us to believe in a great God, a mighty Saviour and an all-wise Spirit to guide us.

We ask all in the name of Jesus Christ our Saviour and Lord,

Amen

January 26, 1975

Help us, our Father,
As we seek to maintain the unity of the Spirit in the bond of peace to remember that if we are close to Thee we cannot be far from one another. Help us to remember when we seek to be in unity with other people that we can find that unity in loyalty to Jesus Christ better than any other way. Dismiss us with Thy blessing and Thy benediction, we pray Thee.
In Jesus' name,

Amen

February 2, 1975

Our Father who art in heaven,
And who art on earth with us, since we are assured that every true Christian is a member of the Body of Christ, help us, each personally, to seek earnestly to know what Thy will is for us to do, what our function is in the body of Christ, and to perform that function faithfully and as skillfully as we are able, with all the help we can get. Go with us to our homes, we pray Thee, be with us that we may do Thy will and advance Thy Kingdom in our part of the world.
For Jesus' sake,

Amen

On Saturday, March 15, 1975, Levi T. Pennington entered the Newberg Community Hospital with the symptoms of a cold. On Monday morning, only two days later, his physical strength quietly and peacefully surrendered to the inexorable demands of the Eternal.

Notes to Chapter VI

1. University of Oregon Collection (UOC).
2. (UOC).
3. (UOC).
4. Family Papers (FP).
5. (FP).
6. From the Benedictions collected by Mr. and Mrs. Frank Cole, preserved in Shambaugh Library.

Sources
Consulted

PUBLISHED MATERIALS

The sources given in the following section are provided for a reader to know the direct resource for specific attitudes reflected in the study and for specific dates and other data. Broad and general backgrounds are not included in the interest of presenting an unencumbered bibliography.

Among the many artists who have provided studies of American moods and periods, the works of two were influential in attempting to capture a spirit of the turn of the century: *Frederic Remington, Paintings, Drawings, and Sculpture*, edited by Peter H. Hassrick (Published by Harry N. Abrams, Inc., in Association with the Amon Carter Museum of Western Art); and *Thomas Hart Benton*, text by Matthew Baigell, also a New Concise NAL Edition.

For understanding Dr. Pennington's training in oratory four sources were depended upon: John Quincy Adams, *Lectures on Rhetoric and Oratory* (N.Y.: Russell & Russell, 1962), in two volumes; John Franklin Genung, *The Working Principles of Rhetoric* (Boston: Ginn & Company, 1900); Chauncey Allen Goodrich, *Essays from Select British Eloquence* (Kingsport: Southern Illinois University Press, 1963); and Karl R. Wallace, *History of Speech Education* in America (N.Y.: Appleton-Century-Crofts, 1954).

Although many of Levi Pennington's essays and sermons were published, they were read in manuscript in nearly all cases, as were his poems. Both manuscript and published editions of his autobiography were consulted under the title, *Rambling Recollections of Ninety Happy Years* (Portland: Metropolitan Press, 1967). This is, as suggested by the title, a recollection and does not provide dates or a dependable chronology; it is a useful tool for understanding his interests.

Those resources most frequently consulted in establishing data on the history of Pacific College and Oregon Yearly Meeting were, in addition to college bulletins and Yearly Meeting programs: Veldon J. Diment, *The First Fifty Years* (1941, Published by the Authority of the Board of Managers), a history of Pacific College; Ralph K. Beebe, *A Garden of the Lord* (Newberg: The Barclay Press, 1968), a history of Oregon Yearly Meeting which contains very helpful data on officials, monthly meetings, and the college; and the *Constitution and Discipline for Oregon Yearly Meeting of Friends Church*, 1911, and the revised *Constitution* adopted June, 1945. If information obtained from individuals or written sources did not agree, or if the original, signed document could not be used, the actions, dates, and specific data given in the *Oregon Yearly Meeting Minutes* were considered accurate. The same principle was used regarding information for other yearly meetings and for the Five Years Meeting.

UNPUBLISHED MATERIALS

A great many impressions and judgments came from knowing Dr. Pennington from 1950 until his death in 1975. Five years of this quarter century were spent in Newberg as Academic Dean of George Fox College, with frequent association with him in Rotary Club, church, and other occasions. However there was no thought during this time of undertaking to write his biography.

Conversations and interviews with selected people served as guides to significant events and sources of information. These included his former students, co-workers in the church, children of his personal friends, and members of the Pennington family.

Shambaugh Library of George Fox College houses a large collection of both published and unpublished materials concerning the history and writing of the Quakers. It also is now the repository for the private papers of many Quaker leaders in the Pacific Northwest; its museum and other Quaker memorabilia, together with its file of newpapers of the area, served as a resource for tracing a number of stories.

The Pennington Papers were the mine from which the greatest amount of information was brought to the surface. Reference to these items is given in the text and in notes. The location of these materials is provided in the notes at the end of each chapter by using the following symbols for each collection: UOC—The Pennington Papers procured and organized by the University of Oregon, now on permanent loan to George Fox College; this collection includes diaries, addresses, graduate school papers, unpublished manuscripts, and over 100,000 letters, both incoming and outgoing. SL—Shambaugh Library Quaker Collection. FP—Personal Family papers yet to be organized and assigned to a library collection consisting of many letters, school records, diaries, addresses and sermons, and material from the press. EE—the Errol Elliott file of original correspondence containing information intended for a Pennington biography. All Minutes from Quaker church bodies cited in the study are from the Shambaugh Collection.

Index

Compiled by the author.

This index may appear too full for a work of this length. Because of its length, an explanation of some principles used in forming headings may be useful. An effort has been made to aid a reader by using subheadings to indicate the aspects of many topics included.

To avoid needless repetition, only a few headings are used for the name *Levi T. Pennington*, and for Oregon Yearly Meeting. When these occur only the abbreviations LTP and OYM are used in subheadings.

Bis after a reference number denotes that the item is alluded to twice quite separately on the same page of the text; *n* stands for note; *q* for quotation.

The alphabetical arrangement is word by word.

well as by the inspiration
of your fine influence, that
I do any worth while thing
which I ever accomplish.

You cannot imagine,
dear lady, how I long
to be able to tell you con-
vincingly of my appreci-
ation of all the help you
have given me all the
years since you hon-
ored me by becoming
my wife. The care of my-
self and my children, the
help you gave me in the
work I tried to do for
the church, the aid
you gave me in work-
ing my way through
college, and all the
invaluable help you